Introduction

The January 2006 legislative election victory of HAMAS (*Harakat al-Muqawama al Islamiyya* –

the Islamic Resistance Movement) seemed to turn US President George W. Bush's policy "to actively

work to bring the hope of democracy, development, free markets, and free trade to every corner of the

world" on its ear.[1] In the aftermath of the election the administration indicated that it would not work

with a government that included terrorists. Israel reacted in a similar manner. The European Union soon

followed suit, refusing to work with the fledgling Palestinian government. These actions made it

impossible for HAMAS and President Mahmoud Abbas, a member of the FATAH (*Harakat al-Tahrir al-*

Watani al-Filastini – The Palestinian National Liberation Movement), to rule Palestine through the

National Unity Government.[2] The Palestinian President dissolved the Parliament, and anarchy erupted in

Gaza. Determined to consolidate its electoral gains, HAMAS forcefully evicted FATAH from the Gaza

strip. In one election, the Palestinians were able to do what the Israelis had failed to do in over three

decades of counter –insurgency operations, split the Palestinians into West Bank and Gaza Factions.[3]

---

[1] George W. Bush, *The National Security Strategy of the United States of America.* Washington, DC. National Security Council, September 2002. http://www.whitehouse.gov/nsc/nss.html (accessed April 4, 2007). According to polls HAMAS continues to enjoy support of the Palestinian people. HAMAS received 44% of the overall votes cast in the February 2006 election. See: Bernard Gwertzman, "Shikaki: Palestinians Support Hamas, But Most Favor Negotiated Peace with Israel" Council on Foreign Relations, (September 25, 2006): http://www.cfr.org/publication/11522/. (accessed October 9, 2008). While support for HAMAS has ebbed and flowed since the election, a survey indicated that HAMAS had 35% overall Palestinian support over its rival FATAH, with 40% support in Gaza and 31% in the FATAH controlled West Bank as of March 2008. See Palestinian Center for Policy and Survey Research - Survey Research Unit. "Palestinian Public Opinion Poll No (27)." Palestinian Center for Policy and Survey Research. http://www.pcpsr.org/survey/polls/2008/p27epressrelease.html (accessed July 24, 2008).

[2] FATAH is the dominant of the (approximately) twelve political parties of the Palestinian Liberation Organization (PLO). Under Yasser Arafat, FATAH assumed control of the PLO in 1969 and has maintained control since then. In 2004 under the Oslo Accords, the PLO effectively became the Palestinian National Authority.

[3] Israel has historically used HAMAS as a counterbalance to the PLO. See: Richard Sale, "Hamas History Tied to Israel," UPI, June 18, 2002, http://www.informationclearinghouse.info/article10456.htm (accessed October 4, 2008). This article states that Israel provided both direct and indirect funds to the Muslim Brotherhood in Palestine and HAMAS in an effort to weaken the PLO. This accusation is repeated by Mahmood Mamdani, *Good Muslim, Bad Muslim* (New York: Pantheon Books, 2004), 121. See also: Hisham H. Ahmad, *Hamas: From Religious Salvation to Political Transformation: The Rise of Hamas in Palestinian Society* (Jerusalem, Israel: PASSIA, 1994), 33 and Karen Armstrong, *The Battle for God: A History of Fundamentalism* (New York: Ballantine Publishing, 2000), 368. Ahmad and and Armstrong indicate that Israeli officials acquiesced to the formation of HAMAS as a counterbalance to the PLO.

1

Could an approach based on a deeper understanding of the organizations involved have resulted in a better outcome for the Palestinians, Israel, and the United States? This monograph will show that the application of constructivist theory could result in a better understanding of and thus a more effective US policy towards HAMAS and possibly similar organizations. The 2006 National Security Strategy (NSS) established that "it is the policy of the United States to seek and support democratic movements and institutions in every nation and culture, with the ultimate goal of ending tyranny in our world."[4] Given this position, this monograph will recommend a strategy that is consistent with this policy in a location that is critical to the interest of the US.

The 2006 election of HAMAS presents an opportunity for the US to bring resolution to the Israeli-Palestinian issue. The 2002 NSS stated: "The Israeli-Palestinian conflict is critical because of the toll of human suffering, because of America's close relationship with the state of Israel, and key Arab states, and because of the regions importance to other global priorities of the United States."[5] HAMAS is important to US foreign policy interests in the Middle East for other reasons. HAMAS controls the Gaza Strip, which is wedged between two US allies in the Global War on Terror (GWOT), Egypt and Israel.[6] An ungoverned or misgoverned Gaza strip could allow for the unimpeded flow of arms into the area to be used against Israel. Another potential problem with instability in Gaza is the movement of those opposed to the Egyptian government from or through the Palestinian territories into Egypt. The current elected majority party in the Palestinian Legislature, HAMAS, is considered by the United States to be a terrorist

---

[4] George W. Bush, *The National Security Strategy of the United States of America*. Washington, DC. National Security Council, March 2006. http://www.whitehouse.gov/nsc/nss/2006/ (accessed April 4, 2007), 6.

[5] Bush, 2002, 14.

[6] Gaza is 360 square kilometers with a population of 1,482,405 and a growth rate of 3.6%. Its birth rate is 5.64 children per woman. For perspective, Gaza is approximately the size of the US Virgin Islands, with a population growth rate that would place it in the top four countries in the world, and a birth rate that is in the top fifteen. See Index Mundi, "Gaza Strip Demographics Profile," Index Mundi, http://www.indexmundi.com/gaza_strip/demographics_profile.html (accessed August 8, 2008); Knowledge Rush, "Demographics of the Gaza Strip," Knowledge Rush, http://www.knowledgerush.com/kr/encyclopedia/Demographics_of_the_Gaza_Strip/ (accessed August 8, 2008); and The Economist, *Pocket World in Figures*, 2008 ed. (London: Profile Books).

organization.[7] Palestine is one of the few examples of a democracy in the Middle East. Moreover, HAMAS is critical because relations with this organization could set precedents for future policy and US government action. HAMAS is the first *Salafist* political party to assume a leadership role as a government since the fall of the Taliban in Afghanistan. Policies developed by the US in dealing with HAMAS may set precedence for future action, should similar events occur in the Islamic World.[8]

The election of HAMAS can be viewed as another example of the legitimization of fundamental political Islam following the election of Hezbollah to seats in the Lebanese legislature. Karen Armstrong, John Esposito, and many others have identified and examined Islam's movement towards fundamentalism; this monograph will limit its scope relative to HAMAS. The Resistance Movement came to power owing to several factors.[9] The failings and shortcomings of the secular FATAH party presented HAMAS with an opportunity. The party founded by Yasser Arafat and led by Mahmoud Abbas failed to use the Palestinian Authority to provide effective governance to Palestine in general and Gaza in particular. Much of the world perceived it as corrupt and inept.[10] The Palestinian people and much of the people of the Middle East, in contrast, perceive HAMAS as incorruptible. They serve as a welcome replacement for the corruption and cronyism of FATAH, which had bled the Palestinian coffers dry.[11] HAMAS has effectively combined a message of resistance against Israeli oppression and services geared to improving the everyday existence of Palestinians with the perception that they are

---

[7] U.S. Department of State, "Foreign Terrorist Organizations (as of 12/30/2004)," http://www.state.gov/documents/organization/41055.pdf (accessed June1, 2008).

[8] Chris Heffelfinger, "Hamas' Victory and the Future of Democracy in the Middle East," The Arab Washingtonian, http://www.arabwashingtonian.org/english/article.php?issue=2&articleID=15 (accessed October 6, 2008). Heffelfinger is a researcher associated with the US Military Academy's Counterterrorism Center and The Jamestown Foundation, a counterterrorist think-tank. He argues that US reaction to the HAMAS election will set a precedent for democracy promotion in the Middle East.

[9] See Karen Armstrong, *The Battle for God: A History of Fundamentalism* (New York: Ballantine Publishing, 2000) or John L. Esposito, *Unholy War: Terror in the Name of Islam* (Oxford, England: Oxford University Press, 2002).

[10] Matthew Levitt, *HAMAS: Politics, Charity, and Terrorism in the Service of Jihad* (New Haven, CT: Yale University Press, 2006): 1. Despite this, Mahmoud Abbas the leader of FATAH since the death of Arafat was elected President by a landslide in January 2005.

[11] Ayoob, *The Many Face of Political Islam: Religion and Politics in the Muslim World* (Ann Arbor, MI: University of Michigan Press, 2008), 20 and Levitt, 1.

incorruptible.[12] This allowed an organization that is largely identified in the West as one dedicated to terrorism to win a landslide victory in the Palestinian Legislative election.

The United States' ability to develop an effective policy to deal with democratically elected, yet ideologically hostile, governments is a requirement. The US needs this to reestablish itself as an effective actor in the Muslim world. Islamic parties continue to play a role in much of the Islamic World. The AKP party currently controls Turkey, Hezbollah is represented in the Lebanese parliament and effectively controls Southern Lebanon, and Islamic political parties play a large role in Indonesia.[13] While the Gaza strip may seem inconsequential to the foreign policy of the United States based on the fact that it barely registers as a policy concern of the average American, the electoral success of an organization designated by the US State Department as a supporter of terrorism may be a sign of things to come. In the few Muslim countries that have democratically chosen leadership, religiously based organizations continue to assume leadership. Clearly the differences between AKP and HAMAS are greater than the similarities, however the election of both is indicative of the growing popularity of Islamic parties in the Muslim World. The development of an effective policy to deal with HAMAS will better position the United States to fight the GWOT and, more importantly, win the war of ideas in the Muslim world.

There are three parts to this paper. The first part describes constructivist theory and its relevance to international relations. The second part applies this theory to an analysis of HAMAS. This examination will suggest that a better understanding of the nature of the organization could lead to a more informed and productive policy. Constructivist theory will be applied to facilitate a better understanding of HAMAS' behavior in the past, predict a range of potential actions in the future, and ultimately recommend a strategy to deal with the organization. The examination will reveal an organization that is undergoing a change in identity and norms. The final section will make recommendations suggesting how the US should deal with HAMAS based on the its potential to change. These recommendations will

---

[12] Levitt, 238.

[13] Ayoob, 21.

be informed by examples of how a policy based on an understanding of an adversary's normative structure will better inform strategic policy decisions

Constructivist Theory - Norms and Identity

Constructivist theory attempts to explain the behavior of international actors through an examination of their normative structures, interests, means, and behaviors.[14] The constructivist approach was developed at the end of the Cold War to elucidate the growing importance of the role of identity and ideas in explaining action.[15] It borrows heavily from sociology but is informed by both ethnography and anthropology. Of particular importance to the theory is the normative structure and its role in interest formation, instrumentality or means selection, and resulting behavior.[16] Normative Structure is a two-part construct that consists of behavioral norms and actor identity. The interaction of self-perception and how an actor determines what is right and wrong affects and is affected by interests, means, and behaviors. For constructivists "ideas are not merely rules or "road maps" for action, but rather ideas operate "all the way down" to actually shape actors and action in world politics. In other words, when ideas are norms, they not only constrain actors, but also constitute actors and enable action."[17]

Constructivist theory is the newest of the three major approaches to international relationships theory. The others are referred to as the realist and liberal theories. None of these approaches are monolithic or dominated by any single theorist. They can, however, be summarized in general terms.

---

[14]. See – Ted Hopf, "The Promise of Constructivism in International Relations Theory," *International Security* 23, no. 1 (Summer 1998): 196 http://www.jstor.org/stable/2539267 (accessed July 22, 2008). Hopf, citing the work of Kratochwil, points out that constructivism is an approach, not a theory. This monograph uses the terms interchangeable as a matter of convenience.

[15] Stephen M. Walt, "International Relations: One World, Many Theories". *Foreign Policy*, no. 110. Special Edition: Frontiers of Knowledge (Spring, 1998): 41, http://ic.ucsc.edu/~rlipsch/pol160A/Walt.1998.pdf (accessed October 4, 2008).

[16] Theo Farrell, "Constructivist Security Studies: Portrait of a Research Program". International Studies Review 4, no. 1, (Spring 2002): 49, http://www.jstor.org/stable/3186274 (accessed July 21, 2008). See also Hopf, 172. For an interesting historical application see Richard Ned Lebow, "Thucydides the Constructivist". The American Political Science Review 95, no. 3 (September 2001): 558, http://www.jstor.org/stable/3118232 (accessed July 21, 2008).

[17] Farrell, 50.

Stephen Walt, professor of International Relations at Harvard's John F. Kennedy School of Governance, asserts that the realist approach:

> ...depicts international affairs as a struggle for power among self-interested states and is generally pessimistic about the prospects for eliminating conflict and war. Realism dominated the Cold War years because it provided simple but powerful explanations for war, alliances, imperialism, obstacles to cooperation, and other international phenomena...[18]

Another way that social scientists have framed issues within international relations is referred to as the liberal approach. According to Andrew Moravcsik, professor of politics and international affairs at Princeton University, "liberal IR theory elaborates the insight that state-society relations – the relationship of states to domestic and transnational social context in which they are embedded have a fundamental impact on state behavior in world politics."[19] It is important to be aware of this theory because it has shaped the formation of many international organizations. The liberal perspective focuses on how a state's interests are influenced by engagement with its people and other states. Liberal theories emphasize cooperation amongst states and the role of international organizations. The theory examines how behavior is influenced by cooperation and interaction. The realist approach emphasizes power and its relation to the state. Neither the realist nor liberal theories can easily or completely explain the organization and actions of groups such as HAMAS. The realist model cannot explain why HAMAS stubbornly clings to its refusal to recognize Israel's right to exist. The liberal approach fails to fully explain the lack of success international organizations have had in resolving the Israel-Palestine issue, despite years of international organization involvement. The advantage of the Constructivist approach is that it holds the promise of greater explanatory power than the realist and liberal theories, particularly in relation to a group such as HAMAS. The Resistance Movement spends significant amounts of energy defining its organization, beliefs, and tactics. Unlike realist theory, that assumes that all states are

---

[18] Stephen M. Walt, "International Relations: One World, Many Theories," *Foreign Policy*, no. 110. Special Edition: Frontiers of Knowledge (Spring, 1998): 31 http://ic.ucsc.edu/~rlipsch/pol160A/Walt.1998.pdf (accessed October 4, 2008).

[19] Andrew Moravcsik, "Taking Preferences Seriously: A Liberal Theory of International Politics," *International Organization* 51, no. 4 (Autumn, 1997): 513 http://www.jstor.org/stable/2703498 (accessed October 6, 2008).

homogenous in their normative structures and means, a constructivist approach assumes that identities, norms, interests are both fluid and varied. A constructivist approach offers insights because it speaks to the central issue of HAMAS, its identity and behavioral norms.[20]

Despite the appropriateness of constructivist theory in an examination of HAMAS, it does have some limitations. Theorist Paul Kowert and Jeffrey Legro identified some of them.[21] One of the difficulties is norm identification. It is difficult to distinguish between an individual and group norm, or at least to identify the point at which an individual norm becomes a group norm. However, it is not necessary to pinpoint the exact point of collectivization but rather to focus on identification. For the purposes of this paper, norms will be identified using what international relations theorist Theo Farrell terms "physical residues". These are the means by which norms are codified and expressed to the rank and file members of an organization, its sponsors, and constituents.[22] A related problem with the application of constructivist theory is that currently there is no quantifiable measure of norm strength in international relations.[23] It is difficult to discern what norm will take precedence when norms diverge.

The identification problem's opposite is the ubiquitous nature of norms, what Kowert and Legro refer to as the "embarrassment of norms".[24] They explain this issue as

> An equally troubling issue for those working in the sociological tradition is not the
> difficulty of identifying norms but their ubiquity. Several of the empirical essays in this

---

[20] Ronald L. Jepperson, Alexander Wendt, and Peter J. Katzenstein, "Norms, Identity, and Culture in National Security," in *The Culture of National Security: Norms and Identity in World Politics*, ed. Peter J. Katzenstein (New York: Columbia University Press, 1996), 33-37. The centrality of HAMAS's identity as both Islamic and as a resistance movement is discussed in Loren D. Lyberger, *Identity and Religion in Palestine* (Princeton, NJ: Princeton University Press, 2007), 84-85.

[21] Paul Kowert and Jeffrey Legro, "Norms, Identity, and Their Limits: A Theoretical Reprise," in *The Culture of National Security: Norms and Identity in World Politics*, ed. Peter J. Katzenstein (New York: Columbia University Press, 1996), 483. For the purposes of this monograph only those that are applicable to the specific case of HAMAS will be discussed here.

[22] Farrell, 60.

[23] There is research on measuring social norms, however, this is limited to sociology and has not been applied to international relations. See – Colin F. Camerer and Ernst Fehr, "Measuring Social Norms and Preferences Using Experimental Games: A Guide for Social Scientists" (working papers series no. 91, University of Zurich, January, 2002), http://papers.ssrn.com/sol3/papers.cfm?abstract_id=299143 (accessed August 7, 2008).

[24] Kowert and Legro, 486.

7

volume make it clear that norms are multifaceted and that many different identities can exist side by side in a collectivity.[25]

Nearly any behavior can be explained by referring to norms. Another effect of the embarrassment of norms is that norms tend to have descriptive utility rather than predictive strength. Legro developed an approach to better identify influential norms and to help researchers to determine which norms will take precedence when they conflict. The process involves determining which norms are clearly codified, which ones have withstood the test of time, and which appear to be universally accepted by the group.[26] Clear codification allows for the identification of norms that have been consistently written or expressed. Durability speaks to two aspects of a particular norm, its ability to withstand pressure to change and the amount of time that it has been present. Acceptance speaks to how broadly the norm is adopted within the group. In order to better explain these issues, an example may better elucidate the concepts. In February 2006 HAMAS offered Israel a *Hudna* (temporary ceasefire).[27] This behavior seems to conflict with the Resistance Movement's stated norm that "there is no solution for the Palestinian question except through Jihad. Initiatives, proposals and international conferences are all a waste of time and vain endeavors."[28] Despite this, shortly after the 2006 election a HAMAS leader has also stated that negotiation is not out of the question.[29] Also, 51% of Palestinian HAMAS supporters and 2/3 of Palestinians support a political settlement with Israel.[30] In June 2008 a *Hudna* was agreed upon

---

[25] Kowert and Legro, 486.

[26] Paul Legro cited in Farrell, 61.

[27] Robert Spencer explains the concept of Hudna in the context of Islamic law: "The Shafi'i school of Islamic jurisprudence stipulates that there must be "some interest served in making a truce other than mere preservation of the status quo." The only "interests that justify making a truce are such things as Muslim weakness because of lack of numbers or materiel" — which the time of the truce would allow the Muslim forces to remedy — "or the hope of an enemy becoming Muslim" ('Umdat al-Salik, o9.16)." Robert Spencer, "Mark Levine: Noam Chomsky as Rock Star," FrontPageMagazine.com, http://frontpagemag.com/Articles/Read.aspx?GUID=4F4BF775-1098-4A19-BBFC-C529E0AD76DA (accessed October 14, 2008).

[28] HAMAS. August 1998. *The Covenant of the Islamic Resistance Movement.* Article 13. http://www.yale.edu/lawweb/avalon/mideast/hamas.htm (accessed February 5, 2008).

[29] The Associated Press, "Hamas Leader: Negotiations 'Not Taboo'," *The Jerusalem Post*, January 24, 2006. http://www.jpost.com/servlet/Satellite?cid=1137605897469&pagename=JPost%2FJPArticle%2FShowFull (accessed October 7, 2008).

[30] Khalil Shikaki, "With Hamas in Power: Impact of Palestinian Domestic Developments on

between Israel and HAMAS.[31] Using Legro's test for norms of codification, durability, and acceptance, the prohibition against negotiation is clearly codified in the *Covenant*, the foundational document of HAMAS. The fact that HAMAS has never openly acknowledged negotiation with Israel points to its durability. However, the election of HAMAS has placed the organization under pressure to respond to the demands of the people. The fact that Palestinian's support negotiation combined with the desire to lead the Palestinian people may have forced HAMAS to modify this norm. A one-time norm may no longer be acceptable to the body of HAMAS.

Another potential challenge in the application of a constructivist approach is that norms account for both continuity and change.[32] Researchers have identified norms as a source of change, these norms and thus behaviors may change as a result of a shock to the system. At the same time, there are historical examples that illustrate cases in which norms were reinforced by a shock to the system.[33] Finally, the constructivist approach requires some assumptions relative to the role of agency in actor behavior. Simply put, do normative structures determine actor actions or to actors shape normative structures? This issue points to the fact that political actors may manipulate group norms and identity in order to achieve their own political ends. This issue will be addressed by considering the consistency of behavior and normative structures over time. While the use of norms in an instrumental fashion may be politically expedient, in the long run behavior should match norms.

As previously mentioned, the constructivist approach consists of an examination of norms, interests, means, and behaviors and how all of these interact with one another. Kowert and Legro describe norms as a two-part construct that they refer to as "normative structure." The parts consist of

---

Options for the Peace Process," *Crown Center Working Papers* 1 (February 2007): 10

[31] Isabel Kershner, "Israel Agrees to Truce with Hamas on Gaza," The New York Times, June 18, 2008. http://www.nytimes.com/2008/06/18/world/middleeast/18mideast.html?hp (accessed October 7, 2008).

[32] Kowert and Legro, 488.

[33] This problem is seen in the varied opinions of HAMAS observers on the effect of the 2006 elections. Some claim that HAMAS will transition from resistance movement to responsible actors while others insist that HAMAS is incapable of change. The author acknowledges this potential problem and attempts to account for this in the final section of the paper (recommendations).

behavioral norms and actor identity.[34] Norms are the measure by which a culture determines what is and is not a proper action. According to Farrell they are "intersubjective beliefs about the social and natural world that define actors, their situations, and the possibilities of action."[35] He explained the powerful role of norms in saying, "when ideas are norms, they not only constrain actors, but also constitute actors and enable action."[36]

Normative structures are developed, maintained, changed, moderated, or mediated by other norms, the environment, social interaction, and internally.[37] Other norms, particularly ones that compete, interact and affect one another. One example of the role of interaction in normative structure formation is the conflict that HAMAS faces between the need to continue the resistance and the simultaneous need to provide its people with good governance and basic services. HAMAS was founded by the Muslim Brotherhood to resist Israeli occupation, with the goal to replace Israel with an Islamic State.[38] Israel and the Quartet have refused to deal with HAMAS and have effectively isolated them in Gaza.[39] This has inhibited HAMAS' ability to provide effective services to the people of Gaza. This tension has caused an existential crisis in the organization that must be resolved.[40] This illustration suggests that normative structure may change. Actions and events such as participation in legislative elections, the election victory, dissolution of the National Unity Government, combined with conflict with Israel and FATAH all reinforce or modify the normative structure of HAMAS.

The environment or ecology in which a nation state is situated also affects norms. The role that Western isolation and Iranian support plays in the identity of HAMAS is an example of how the international environment could potentially affect normative structure. Another aspect of the role of the

---

[34] Kowert and Legro, 453 and 462.

[35] Farrell, 49.

[36] Ibid, 50.

[37] Kowert and Legro, 470.

[38] HAMAS, Articles 2-3 and Ayoob, 120.

[39] The Quartet refers to the United Nations, Russia, the European Union, and the United States.

[40] Shikaki, 7-10.

environment in norm development and change is how they are modified by system shocks.[41] System

shocks are those events that loosen a group's commitment to particular norms and identities, providing

proponents of change the opportunity to act.[42] System shocks, such as those experienced by HAMAS in

the election victory of 2006 are often used to explain changes in norms.

The social process of norm formation is divided between the concept of social diffusion and

interaction role theory.[43] Social diffusion is the concept of norm development through interaction. This

phenomenon is seen when state actors participate in international or interstate or negotiations.[44] This

participation results in the development or modification of norms. For example, the choice of Israel to

reject direct negotiates with HAMAS affects the development and modification of that group's norms.

The concept of norm development through interaction holds that norms are developed through the process

of identification of in-groups and out-groups. Following this line of thought, norms are developed when a

group juxtaposes itself against another. The process of interaction with an out-group modifies what is

considered to be either positive or negative behavior. This could be seen in the history of interaction

between FATAH and HAMAS. *The Covenant of the Islamic Resistance Movement* refers to the PLO as

brothers in the resistance. Years of competition and negative interaction seem to have weakened this

sense of fraternity. This evolution may have contributed to the apparent ease both parties demonstrated in

adopting violence, unjust imprisoning, and torture in the aftermath of the 2006 elections.[45] Internal

---

[41] The example most constructivist literature points to is the effect WWII had on the normative structures of both Germany and Japan.

[42] Kowert and Legro, 473.; Annika Bjrkdahl, "Norms in International Relations: Some Conceptual and Methodological Reflections," Cambridge Review of International Affairs15, no. 1 (April 2002): 17.

[43] Kowert and Legro, 474 & 475.

[44] There are obvious connections to liberal international relations theory. However, liberal theory is more concerned with how this interaction effects behavior whereas the constructivist approach is more concerned with how these interactions affect normative structures.

[45] Ravi Nessman, "Hamas Gunmen Battle Fatah Police in Gaza," The Associated Press, May 22, 2006, http://www.washingtonpost.com/wp-dyn/content/article/2006/05/22/AR2006052200159.html (accessed October 5, 2008); CBS News and Associated Press, "Fears Of A Palestinian Civil War Grow," CBS News, May 22, 2006, http://www.cbsnews.com/stories/2006/05/22/world/main1639950.shtml (accessed October 5, 2008); The Associated Press, "Hamas accuses Fatah strongman in Haniyeh assassination attempt, inflaming tensions," The Associated

processes refer to the diffusion of norms from the individual to the group. This concept is used in the analysis of the role language plays a role in the development of norms. Dartmouth Professor of Government Richard Lebow explained this concept in the following manner "To understand their behavior and the social context that enables it, we need to track the ways in which words acquire, hold, or lose meanings and how news meanings arise and spread."[46] Both interaction and the environment affect the normative structure.

Behavioral norms combined with identity are the key components of what constructivist theorists refer to as normative structure. According to political scientist Alexander Wendt, identity is a set of meanings that an actor attributes to itself in relationship to others.[47] Professor Ted Hopf explains the role of identity, "In telling you who you are, identities strongly imply a particular set of interests or preferences with respect to choices of action in particular domains, and with respect to particular actors."[48] Identity establishes a minimum level of predictability.[49] Identity is required in order to bring a consistency of expectations to both personal and interstate relations. It gives an "… understanding of other states, its nature, motives, interests, probable actions, attitudes, and role in any given political context."[50] Identity is unconsciously developed in comparison to the other. State identities are a product of both international and domestic interactions.[51] The international community shapes a state's identity by recognizing legitimacy and acting as a gatekeeper for membership in international organizations.[52]

Press, December 14, 2006, http://www.iht.com/articles/ap/2006/12/15/africa/ME_GEN_Israel_Palestinians.php (accessed October 5, 2008).

[46] Lebow, 548.

[47] Alexander, Wendt, "Collective Identity Formation and the International State," *The American Political Science Review* 88, no. 2 (June 1994): 385, http://www.jstor.org/stable/2944711 (accessed October 5, 2008).

[48] Hopf, 175.

[49] Hopf, 174.

[50] Ibid, 193.

[51] Wendt, 385-386 and Peter J. Katzenstein, "Introduction: Alternative Perspectives on National Security," in *The Culture of National Security: Norms and Identity in World Politics*, ed. Peter J. Katzenstein (New York: Columbia University Press, 1996), 24.

[52] Katzenstein, "Introduction", 24.

Domestic interactions effect identity through the process of legitimization and support. How a state addresses these issues impacts on that state's identity. HAMAS as a governing body will be expected by the Palestinian people to govern efficiently and effectively, or at the very least more efficiently and effectively than the former regime under Yasser Arafat.[53] The people's expectations of the majority party in the legislature may be different than their expectations of HAMAS as a resistance movement. This indicates two potential sources of identity conflict.[54] The first is through competition of definitions that call for conflicting behaviors. This conflict is particularly salient for a discussion of HAMAS while it transitions from the role of resistance movement to that of a ruling political party. The second also applies to HAMAS. It is identity conflict that is caused by a change in historical conditions. This conflict impacts on the organizations ability to maintain its narrative and may ultimately result in changes in behavior. The combination of identity and behavioral norms forms the normative construct. This construct determines interests.

Interests are determined by the normative structure. According to Hopf, interests are the "… products of the social practices that mutually constitute actors and structures."[55] An organization, individual, or state will act in a manner that is consistent with its identity.[56] If a group's identity is that of a resistance movement it will behave as a resistance movement. Along those same lines, if a group's identity is that of a ruling political party, it can be expected to behave as a ruling political party.

---

[53] See Khalil Shikaki, "Understanding the Outcome of Palestinian Elections," Arab Media Internet Network, January 28, 2006, http://www.amin.org/look/amin/en.tpl?IdLanguage=1&IdPublication=7&NrArticle=36082&NrIssue=1&NrSection=3 (accessed October 5, 2008).

[54] Michael N. Barnett, "Identity and Alliances in the Middle East," in *The Culture of National Security: Norms and Identity in World Politics*, ed. Peter J. Katzenstein (New York: Columbia University Press, 1996), 411 & 412.

[55] Hopf, 176.

[56] It should be noted that international relations (IR) theorists in general, and constructivists in particular, do not claim that any of the three major IR theories is capable of predicting aberrant behavior. However, most constructivists would argue that their approach identifies potential behaviors that both liberal and realist theoreticians would consider aberrant.

Constructivist theory is also interested in so-called "missing interests".[57] These are interests that a state structure does not have based on its identity. Interests are determined by the normative structure. The interaction of the normative structure with interests determines acceptable means.

Means are the way that interests are connected with behaviors.[58] They are defined as the instruments or policies that are used to accomplish an end. The normative structure affects means by determining their appropriateness and acceptability.[59] Influenced by the normative structure and shaped by interests, means are the final step until observable behavior occurs. The choice of HAMAS to deny Israel's right to exist is confusing only when one does not understand that this refusal is part of its normative structure. One of the demands of the Quartet is that HAMAS recognize Israel's right to exist. This recognition would likely usher in the support of the international community to both HAMAS and the people of Gaza. However, the Resistance Movement's normative structure will not allow for recognition. *The Covenant* codifies Palestine as a *waqf*, land that is holy and ordained by God for the Muslim people.[60] Recognition of Israel would constitute acceptance of Israel occupying what HAMAS considers Muslim holy land. Finally, HAMAS' refusal to recognize Israel has enjoyed the support of a majority of Palestinians.[61] Legro's test for norms - codification, durability, and acceptance - indicates that recognition is unlikely. HAMAS' current normative structure will not allow it to recognize Israel's right to exist.

---

[57] Hopf, 176.

[58] Peter J. Katzenstein, Robert O. Keohane, and Stephen D. Krasner, "International Organization and the Study of World Politics," *International Organization* 52, no. 4, International Organization at Fifty: Exploration and Contestation in the Study of World Politics (Autumn, 1998): 679 http://www.irchina.org/Katzenstein/KKK1998.pdf (accessed 15 October 2008) and Kowert and Legro, 463.

[59] Kowert and Legro, 463-464.

[60] HAMAS, Article 11. See also Glenn E. Robinson, "Hamas as a Social Movement," in *Islamic Activism: A Social Movement Theory Approach*, ed. Quintan Wiktorowicz (Bloomington, IN: University of Indiana Press, 2004), 130.

[61] Shikaki, 8

Behavior is the product of normative structures, interests, and means. For the constructivist, identity and norms can be determined through the observation of consistent behavior.[62] These behaviors become defining. The constructivist approach is circular. An actors actions, behaviors, and practices are based on their identities, norms, and interests. An actors identities, norms, and interests can be inferred from their behavior.[63] The application of the constructivist approach does not require one to assume actor interests, or choice of means. Instead it helps to determine a range of possibility based on actor identity and norms. This determination has the potential to develop policies and strategies that more effectively deal with HAMAS.

HAMAS through a constructivist lens

Behavioral norms and Identity

It is possible to gain insight into the behavioral norms and identity of HAMAS by an examination of their physical manifestations and how others view and interact with them.[64] This examination suggests that HAMAS has defined itself as an independent resistance movement. Also critical to the normative structure is the fact that the Muslim Brotherhood founded it and that it has dedicated itself to the establishment of an Islamic State ruled by *Sharia* through the destruction of the state of Israel. However, events that began with the Oslo accords have worked to create an identity crisis for HAMAS. Since the 2005 run up to the parliamentary elections, the organization began to feel conflicting pressures that worked to both maintain and alter its normative structure. The choice of its leaders to pursue the organization's interests through the ballot box and the electoral victory may signal a change. These events combined with the behaviors of forming a national unity government with FATAH and the governance of Gaza are all events that may signal a change in the normative structure. On the other hand, the dissolution of the National Unity Government, violent establishment of authority over Gaza, and

---

[62] Hopf, 178.

[63] Farrell, 61-62.

[64] By physical manifestations the author means such things as recorded history, writings/pronouncements (particular the Covenant of the Islamic Resistance Movement), published policies, and organization.

international isolation may reinforce what the West considers to be an undesirable normative structure. The following section will examine HAMAS. First it will describe events and interactions that form its identity and behavioral norms. Events such as the organizations foundation and the publication of the Covenant are critical in the establishment of the organization's identity and norms. Interactions with regional and international powers such as Iran, Israel, and the United States have also played a critical role in shaping HAMAS' normative structure. The examination will then look at the Resistance Movement's interests and choice of means. This will focus its change in tactics, such as the choice to participate in elections and the determination to reduce the use of suicide attacks. This section concludes with a brief examination of behaviors that may indicate changes in the normative structure.

The Muslim Brotherhood – The Establishment of the Normative Structure

In order to understand the identity and norms of HAMAS one must first understand the organization that founded it - the Muslim Brotherhood (*Jamiyyat Al-Ikhwan Al-Muslimin*). The Brotherhood provided the ideological underpinnings of HAMAS and ultimately its sense of what HAMAS was to be as an organization. An Egyptian schoolteacher, Hassan al-Banna, founded the Brotherhood in 1928 as a pan-Islamic and *Salafist* movement.[65] Al-Banna held the *Salafist* view that the Muslim world was in decline and that a return to true Islam was required to restore its greatness. Adherents to *Salafism* believe that in order to truly be Islamic, Muslims and their society must return to the beliefs and social order of Muhammad and his contemporaries. Their approach is to use a combination of society, culture, and politics to create an Islamic state as Mohammed had done in his lifetime. The Brotherhood is the oldest and perhaps the most influential of all Salafist organizations. It has inspired many off shoots such as Pakistan's *Jamaat-i-Islami* and served as the ideological impetus for *al-Qaeda* (AQ). Given its pan-Islamic orientation, international focus, and missionary approach the Brotherhood

---

[65] Al-Banna is quoted in the introduction to the Covenant: "Israel will exist and will continue to exist until Islam will obliterate it, just as it obliterated others before it."

has adapted each branch to fit the needs of the local population. However, all branches remain true to set of three central ideas:

> the desire to purify and thus revive Islamic life; the desire to restore the worldly fortunes of Islam; and the conviction that both can be achieved only by reappropriating the model of Islam's seventh-century founders, the Salaf or virtuous ancestors, which include Mohammed and his closest companions or follows [66]

The Brotherhood, in most cases, discourages a violent approach to achieve the establishment of a Muslim state.[67] This later served as a point of departure for the Palestinians from the Egyptian branch.

The Muslim Brotherhood spread to the Palestinian territories in the late 1960s. In 1978 it officially registered with the Israeli government as a nonprofit organization under the name *Moujama*. The Israeli government, happy to take advantage of any opportunity to promote infighting amongst the Palestinians with the establishment of an alternate to the PLO, was initially complicit with the founding of *Moujama*.[68] Until the first *Intifada* and the formation of HAMAS, the Palestinian Brotherhood received its marching orders from Egypt. The Palestinian movement was further reinforced with the philosophy and approach of the Egyptian Brotherhood after the assassination of Anwar Sadat. Following Sadat's death the Egyptian government engaged in a crackdown on the Muslim Brotherhood resulting in a mass deportation of foreign-born Brothers, many of who ended up in Palestine, particularly the Gaza Strip.[69] The Palestinians continued to follow the Egyptian lead until events in Palestine forced their hand.

The Palestinian Muslim Brotherhood founded HAMAS (*Hamas* is translated from Arabic as "zeal") in December 1987 during the first Palestinian uprising (*Intifada*) against Israel. The name of HAMAS has some symbolic value beyond the obvious acronym. The word *Muqawama* is often

---

[66] Hillel Fradkin, "The History and Unwritten Future of Salafism." *Current Trends in Islamist Ideology* 6 (2008): 7.

[67] Graham E. Fuller, *The Future of Political Islam* (New York: Palgrave MacMillan, 2003), 53.

[68] Marvin E. Gettleman and Stuart Schaar, ed., *The Middle East and Islamic World Reader* (New York: Grove Press, 2003), 207.

[69] Boaz Ganor. "Hamas: The Islamic Resistance Movement in the Territories". Jerusalem Center for Public Affairs. (February 2, 1992). http://www.jcpa.org/jl/saa27.htm (accessed May 7, 2008).

translated as resistance in English. In Arabic, the word has the connotation of a struggle without end.[70] This is important because the founders of HAMAS see their struggle as one that can only end with victory. The word choice deliberately implies that the organization is willing to sacrifice for an indefinite time period in order to achieve victory.[71] As the role of HAMAS transitions from that of resistance movement to that of governing party, this distinction may come to also have new meaning. The term *muqawama* speaks to an endless struggle, not necessarily one that is violent. A change in HAMAS' means seems to indicate a change in normative structure.

The founding of a militant arm and the adoption of violence as a tactic to further the struggle against Israel signaled an effective break with the Egyptian Muslim Brotherhood.[72] In the face of the *Intifada*, The Palestinian wing of the Brotherhood realized that it, and thus its beliefs, would lose support to other organizations if it failed to answer the call for a violent struggle against Israel.[73] The support for Islamic Jihad and the PLO skyrocketed during the initial stages of the *Intifada*.[74] The Islamic Jihad was already positioned to exploit the chaos created by the outbreak of mass violence. The PLO was visible enough to make the inaccurate claim that they led the *Intifada*. The Brotherhood carefully weighed the popular support that would be gained from that creation of a militant wing versus the potential cost of being a target of the Israeli security apparatus. The Brotherhood realized that it had obtained operational depth in the twenty years it had operated in the territories. The Israeli security apparatus would be hard pressed to completely eradicate the organization.[75] Under the leadership of Sheikh Ahmed Yassin, the

---

[70] Ehud Yarri, "The Muqawama Doctrine," *Jerusalem Report*, November 13, 2006.

[71] This can be contrasted with FATAH. The decision by FATAH to go with the reverse acronym was due to the fact that *Hataf* is translated from Arabic as "instant death".

[72] Ayoob, 117.

[73] Robinson, 123 and Ahmad, 17.

[74] Wendy Kristianasen, "Challenge and Counterchallenge: Hamas's Response to Oslo,". Journal of Palestine Studies 28, no. 3 (Spring, 1999): 20, http://www.jstor.org/stable/2538305 (accessed May 1, 2008).

[75] It should be noted that Israel did attempt this with the arrest of HAMAS founder and leader Sheikh Ahmed Yassin. This threw the organization into turmoil, but it slowly adapted and took measures to ensure that the organization would continue regardless of the loss of key leaders.

Brotherhood moved ahead with the founding of HAMAS. The new organization rapidly gained popularity and support and eventually subsumed the Brotherhood.[76]

The formation of HAMAS provided it with the foundation of a normative structure, interests, and means. The fact that it was formed as a wing of the Muslim Brotherhood initially imbued it with a religious identity. Also, the departure from the Brotherhood's generally nonviolent approach in response to the demand of the Palestinian people also seems to indicate that HAMAS is practical and responsive to the expressed desire of the people. These two factors seem to indicate an identity that is religiously based yet balanced with pragmatic behavioral norms that select actions that will result in popular support. Israel's domination of the West Bank and Gaza during the First *Intifada*, the effective suppression of Islamic Jihad, combined with the popular demand of the Palestinian people for a violent resistance created a perceived need. The Brotherhood fulfilled this need by founding HAMAS. This also established The Resistance Movement as the religious alternative to the secular PLO.[77] Initially, HAMAS' interests were limited to seizing the leadership role in the first *Intifada*. The nature of the uprising against Israel left violent resistance as the only means that could garner the support of the Palestinian people. The new organization required focus, legitimacy, and the ability to articulate it goals to the people. This was done through the publication of the *Covenant of the Islamic Resistance Movement*.

The Covenant of HAMAS and its meaning – The codification of the normative structure

In 1988 the newly created HAMAS published *The Covenant of the Islamic Resistance Movement* directly challenging the secular PLO for the primary leadership of the Palestinian people in its efforts to destroy Israel and found a Palestinian state in its place. The document was first published August 18, 1988, while the First *Intifada* was still ongoing. It covers a broad series of issues ranging from the conduct of *Jihad* to the role of art in the Resistance. Understanding HAMAS requires a critical examination of *The Covenant*. Scholars differ on its importance of and its actual contribution to the

---

[76] Ahmad, 11.

[77] Ayoob, 117.

normative structure, interests, choice of means, and behaviors. Some interpret it as an antiquated

document that no longer has currency:

> The Hamas Charter or *Al-Mithaq* (the Covenant) was framed in highly religious terms, including various references to the *Qur'an*, the establishment of an Islamic state as a long term goal and well as calling for the destruction of Israel. It is more often cited by the movement's critics than by its leaders/spokesmen. Thus, Hamas initially emerged as a very rigid and inflexible movement. However its later development of a mixed ideology (religious-nationalist) paved the way for both flexibility and pragmatism of Hamas as a political movement.[78]

While others see the Covenant in a different light:

> The Covenant has never been rescinded and the document has never been formally repudiated. In truth, since it is a covenant with Allah, it not only cannot be withdrawn - since it would reflect a breach with a sacred commitment, those in opposition are actually hard-pressed to denounce it inside the *Ummah*. There is no factual basis to argue the apologist narrative - a narrative created for the benefit of a Western audience intellectually crippled by the obsessive demand for "moderate" voices, AS WE UNDERSTAND THE TERM, where none may actually exist.[79]

Regardless of the current role of *The Covenant*, it is the foundational document of the organization and is

critical to a constructivist examination of HAMAS.

The document is divided into a preamble followed by 36 articles; the articles are grouped into

topical areas. The preamble calls on the Islamic world to conduct a *jihad* against Jews and the state of

Israel.[80] It states that HAMAS came into existence when it was needed and the conditions were right for

its creation (i.e. the first *Intifada*). It explains that the Covenant "...clarifies its picture, *reveals its identity*,

---

[78] Michele Pace, "A 'Modern' Islamist Democracy? Perceptions of Democratization in Palestine: the Case of Hamas" (paper presented at the annual conference of the British Society for Middle Eastern Studies, Leeds, England, July 5, 2008).

[79] Stephen Coughlin, e-mail message to author, August 11, 2008. Emphasis is in the original email. Quoted with permission. Other authors seems to take a similar line, "The group's ideology was set forth in its 1988 covenant, which remains operative to this day." Michael Herzog, "Can Hamas Be Tamed?" *Foreign Affairs* 82, no.2 (March/April 2006). http://www.foreignaffairs.org/20060301faessay85207/michael-herzog/can-hamas-be-tamed.html (accessed October 8, 2008).

[80] The Covenant use the word *Jihad* to to imply a "religious struggle", not the overused Western interpretation of "violent struggle". HAMAS, Article 30.

outlines its stand, explains *its aims*, speaks about its hopes, and calls for its support, adoption and joining its ranks."[81]

The first eight articles make up the section entitled "Definition of the Movement". From a constructivist approach, this is, arguably, the most important section of the document. It defines HAMAS as an Islamic movement, which is one of the wings of the Muslim Brotherhood. As such it relies on the teachings of Islam for its guidance. Its goal is to free the oppressed through a pan-Islamic *jihad*. Since it is indeed a religious struggle against non-Muslim oppressors (Israel and the West) all Muslims are obligated to support it.[82] The sixth article of this section focuses the efforts of HAMAS on the liberation of Palestine. This nationalistic focus is one of the critical aspects that separate HAMAS from organizations such as al-Qaeda that focus on the world wide *Umma*. It is the view of HAMAS that the *Umma* is obligated to support them rather than vice versa since Palestine is critical to the Muslim religion.[83] The themes introduced in both the preamble and this section in particular are repeated throughout the document. This first section addresses the concepts of identity and interests. The HAMAS identity was codified as an Islamic movement and as a wing of the Muslim Brotherhood.[84] It also established the liberation of Palestine from Israeli occupation at the organization's primary interest.

After establishing HAMAS' identity *The Covenant* uses two articles to define its objective. That is the establishment of an Islamic state in Palestine. It alludes to the leadership of the secular PLO during the first *Intifada*, "The Islamic Resistance Movement found itself at a time when Islam has disappeared from life."[85] HAMAS fills this void by "...fighting against the false, defeating it and vanquishing it so that justice could prevail, homelands be retrieved, and from its mosques would the voice of the *mu'azen*

---

[81] HAMAS, Introduction. Emphasis added to highlight the fact that the document speaks to the Constructivist concepts of identity and interests.

[82] Ayoob, 117.

[83] Ibid, 118.

[84] Robinson, 131

[85] Hamas, Article 9.

emerge declaring the establishment of the state of Islam…"[86]. This section points to both the identity and interests of HAMAS as an Islamic organization whose goal is the establishment of an Islamic state. HAMAS perceives a clear connection between Islam and the establishment of a Palestinian state. This section makes the connection between a Muslim identity and Palestinian nationalistic interests.

The Strategy and Methods section establishes the means that HAMAS is willing to use in pursuit of its interests. This section also establishes some behavioral norms. Article eleven specifically rejects any territorial compromise; "The Islamic Resistance Movement believes that the land of Palestine is an Islamic *Waqf* consecrated for future Muslim generations until Judgment Day. It, or any part of it, should not be squandered; it, or any part of it, should not be given up."[87] This point is critical because HAMAS does not distinguish between nationalism and religion. In their view Palestinian nationalism and the demands of the Muslim religion are one in the same based on the important role Jerusalem plays in Islam. If one is truly Islamic they must support the struggle for the establishment of an Islamic state in Palestine.[88] The religious message strengthens the call of nationalism in that it not only relates to material gain but also to religious obligation. Articles thirteen through fifteen state that HAMAS refuses any form of negotiation to reach a peaceful solution either directly with the Israelis or as part of an international conference. Final resolution can only be achieved through *jihad* and the only desirable outside assistance is from other Muslims willing to carry this Jihad to the enemy. Article fourteen specifically identifies the circles of obligation to the liberation of Palestine. They are that of Palestinian, Arab, and Muslim. This concept of circles provides an explanation of HAMAS' willingness to work with *Shia* led Iran and Hezbollah. Each has an obligation to support the struggle and they are all inextricably linked. All who fall within these circles are religiously obligated to support the *Jihad* in whatever means possible.

---

[86] Hamas, Article 9.

[87] Ibid, Article Eleven. The term *Waqf* refers to land that has been designated as holy be previous Muslim conquerors. See: Herzog, np; Ahmad, 54.

[88] Brian R. Farmer, *Understanding Radical Islam: Medieval Ideology in the Twenty-First Century* (New York: Peter Lang), 97 and Ahmad, 54-55.

Along with the previously mentioned methods for liberating Palestine, HAMAS dedicated several articles that describe its approach towards developing the Palestinian people as proper Muslims. This is referential to HAMAS' roots in the Muslim Brotherhood, an organization that continues to advocate an approach that emphasizes the development of proper Muslims prior to engaging in *Jihad* to establish the Caliphate. According to Article Sixteen, education should focus on the *Koran* and *Sunna*, the enemy, and current events.[89] Other areas covered are the education of Women and the role of the arts in the struggle to liberate Palestine. Article twenty examines the notion of social responsibility, it also accuses the Jews of attempting to destroy this notion "in a way similar to Nazism..." This is to be countered by the masses facing their enemy as a single body. HAMAS not only asks for the people's support, but also promises to support the people in turn. This section relates to HAMAS's commitment to the people as instruments in the realization of God's will. According to the Covenant's authors it is God's will to return Muslim culture to its Islamic roots and to establish an Islamic state in Palestine.

The final section defines the attitude that HAMAS takes towards Jews, Israel, and to organizations involved in the struggle to liberate Palestine. In articles twenty-two and twenty-eight the Covenant writers seem borderline delusional in their attacks on Israel in particular and Jews in general. They blame Jews for the French and Communist Revolutions as well as World War I and II. Also, they sight the widely discredited and anti-Semitic tract "Protocols of the Elders of Zion" as authoritative.[90] These accusations are so spectacular in their nature that they detract if not negate the overall quality in terms of the *Covenant's* coherence and organization. Article 27 establishes kinship and fraternity with the PLO who share the same goal as HAMAS in the liberation of Palestine from Israel. However, the article is highly critical of the PLO's secular nature, which is not a choice but the result of confusion due to the

---

[89] *Sunna* are the sayings and actions of the prophet not specifically covered in the Koran. While their is debate amongst religious scholars as to their authenticity and origins, Muslims, in general, consider them authoritative.

[90] HAMAS, Article 22. Written in 1903, the *Protocols of the Elders of Zion*, are used by anti-Semites to supposedly prove the claim that Jews have conspired to dominate the world, poison the minds of youth, and spread racial hatred. John S. Curtiss demonstrated that the articles were a forgery in his 1942 work, *An Appraisal of the Protocols of Zion.* See also Robinson, 132.

influx of alternate ideologies.[91] Article 28 warns against spies in infiltrators, problems that plagued both the PLO and other resistance movements. The document concludes with the claim that HAMAS is composed of soldiers who struggle against Zionism, and do not seek glory. Their only goal is the creation of an Islamic state in Palestine. This section relates to the development of identity in comparison to an out-group. In this case, HAMAS is comparing itself to the Jews who they portray as the embodiment of evil and the PLO who is portrayed as brothers or sons who have lost their way.

Not only are the words of *The Covenant* critical, but also the historical context in which it was written. At the time of the publications writing, HAMAS was still an organization on the periphery of the *Intifada*. The Brotherhood chose to form a wing possibly to establish plausible deniability and the ability to easily cut ties should its militant nature become a liability. This would allow the Brotherhood to carry on, should the HAMAS experiment fail. The Muslim Brotherhood also positioned itself to claim any HAMAS successes as theirs. In light of the *Intifada*, bombastic language and the dehumanization of Israel and Jews is to be expected. Given the previous wartime success of Israel and its domination of the territories it is understandable that HAMAS did not see any room for compromise. This was their raison d'être and is based on principles that are historical and non-negotiable for their origin and context. This is what distinguishes HAMAS from secular organizations such as FATAH.

The *Covenant* clearly defined the original normative structure, interests, and means of HAMAS. It established the identity as an Islamic organization that was founded by the Muslim for the purpose of establishing a Palestinian state. The interest of establishing a Palestinian state is embedded in the organization's identity.[92] Later in the document the *Covenant* also states that HAMAS' interest include the establishment of *Sharia* as the law of the land in Palestine.[93] The document also established several behavioral norms. Clearly, it subscribes to the *Salafist* notion of a need to return to the practices of

---

[91] Robinson, 134.

[92] HAMAS, Article 6. "It strives to raise the banner of Allah over every inch of Palestine…"

[93] HAMAS, Article 11. See Ahmad, 56.

Mohammed and his contemporaries.[94] It also establishes the belief that all Muslims are religiously obligated to support their *jihad* to liberate Palestine; failure to do so is sinful and treasonous. Groups such as the PLO are acceptable, because they also struggle against occupation.[95] The land of Palestine is sacrosanct and it cannot be negotiated away. Negotiation in any form is a waste of time.[96] Death is not only acceptable in the furtherance of the group's ends, but also God approves it.[97] The final norm established by the Covenant is the need to serve the people of Palestine and to take care of those not capable to taking care of themselves. This norm undoubtedly is the source for HAMAS' emphasis on the establishment of social services in Palestine, both while out of and in governance. *The Covenant* identifies what means are acceptable to accomplish its interests. The primary means is through *jihad*. HAMAS, like the Muslim Brotherhood, acknowledges the importance preparing Muslims through education and religious training to adopt a Salafist lifestyle as a necessary part of their program.[98] The Covenant established the normative structure of HAMAS; it also identified the organization's interests and some of its acceptable means. The next section will examine how events from the foundation up to the September 11, 2001 attack by *Al Qaeda* on the United States worked to both modify, moderate, and reinforce HAMAS' normative structure, interests, means, and behaviors.

HAMAS – *Intifada* to the Global War on Terror – Modification, Moderation, and Reinforcement of the Normative Structure

The first *Intifada* ended any illusion of the benign occupation that had been the hallmark of Israel's public affairs effort to shape the perception of its activities in Palestine. As the violence spread

---

[94] Ibid, Article 5. "By adopting Islam as its way of life, the Movement goes back to the time of the birth of the Islamic message, of the righteous , for Allah is its target, the Prophet is its example and the Koran is its constitution."

[95] HAMAS, Article 23 and 27.

[96] HAMAS, Article 13. "There is no solution for the Palestinian question except through Jihad. Initiatives, proposals and international conferences are all a waste of time and vain endeavors."

[97] HAMAS, Article 8.

[98] HAMAS, Article 15.

from the disaffected youth of Palestine to the general public, HAMAS, FATAH, and other groups struggled to establish themselves as leaders. Four factors combined to allow for the Islamic Resistance Movement to rapidly expand its influence. The fact that most of the PLO's leaders were no longer in Palestine created an opportunity for HAMAS to establish itself as leaders of the *Intifada* from the ground up. [99] The religious nature of HAMAS positioned it to take advantage of the socioeconomic conditions in Palestine[100] The Territories had similar demographics to other countries that saw the emergence of Islamism.[101] HAMAS' religious and nationalistic message appealed to the disaffected youth of Palestine. Another factor is that Israel moved aggressively to destroy leadership cells of the Islamic Jihad, creating a vacuum that HAMAS was eager to fill.[102] Finally, Israeli authorities initially tolerated the existence of HAMAS as a means to increase tensions between the Palestinian insurgency groups.[103] During this foundational period emphasis was placed on HAMAS' identity as a religiously based organization. They approached their social agenda on three levels, private, social, and political.[104] At the private level, HAMAS appealed to the moral fiber of the Palestinian youth, juxtaposing Islam with what they called the depravity of Judaism. On the social level, they enacted *Sharia* in a manner similar to that seen in Algeria and Iran and later repeated on the streets of Kabul by the Taliban. Unveiled women were brutally punished, as were merchants who sold alcohol. They combined this with the provision of social services.[105] Politically, HAMAS aggressively established themselves in local leadership positions in groups such as trade unions and student groups. These steps enabled HAMAS to become a critical player on the Palestinian political scene. This diversity of approach allowed it to become an organization that

---

[99] Yonah Alexander, *Palestinian Religious Terrorism: Hamas and Islamic Jihad* (Ardsley, NY: Transnational Publishers 2002), 1.

[100] Ahmad, 33.

[101] Gilles Kepel, *Jihad: The Trail of Political Islam*, trans. Anthony F. Roberts, (Cambridge, MA: The Belnap Press of Harvard University, 2002): 154.

[102] See Footnote 3.

[103] Ahmad, 33.

[104] Kepel, 154.

[105] Farmer, 97.

did not rely solely on the on-going *Intifada* to define itself. The events in the early part of the *Intifada* served to reinforce the normative structure of HAMAS. The Palestinian people supported HAMAS based on its religious orientation, nationalistic message, and demonstrated leadership abilities. The First *Intifada* marked the zenith of the organization's religious orientation.

Toward the end of 1988, the PLO declared Palestine to be an independent state while recognizing the right of Israel to exist. In the middle of the *Intifada*, this served as a propaganda coup for HAMAS. In the battle for the hearts and minds of the Palestinian people, they could accuse the PLO of not only lacking Islamic credentials but also of acting as Zionist dupes. Alarmed at the growing popularity of the Islamic Resistance, Israel turned on the group they once believed would serve their purpose of dividing the Palestinian cause. In May 1989 Sheik Ahmad Yassin, the Movement's founder, was imprisoned along with several hundred other key leaders.[106] Having learned from the repression of the Islamic Jihad, the Movement quickly filled the vacuum created with younger men who where closely identified with the *Intifada*.[107] This better positioned HAMAS to carefully craft its message to appeal to the disaffected masses as well as the small but politically sensitive middle class. This time period saw HAMAS' perception of the PLO shift from that of a confused brother to that of a traitor to the Palestinian cause. The interest of HAMAS expanded from solely resisting Israeli occupation to undermining the efforts of the PLO as well.

Despite the crackdown, HAMAS still presented a viable political threat to the PLO. To counter this, they invited the Movement to join the Palestinian National Council. HAMAS, confident in their popularity and the PLO's weakness, demanded a disproportional representation on the council. This was flatly refused, based on the fact that diplomatic progress the PLO had made would be negated by a significant HAMAS representation based on the fact that the resistance movement continued to recognize Israel. The PLO's weakness was compounded by their support of Iraq in the Gulf War of 1990-01. This

---

[106] Alexander, 4 and Ahmad, 36.

[107] Kepel, 156.

cost them critical support from Saudi Arabia and Kuwait. The mass deportation of Palestinians from these countries swelled the population of Palestine with young males who found themselves unemployed. Many of these were attracted to HAMAS.[108] The Resistance Movement's pronouncements during this time period were carefully crafted to ensure that they did not offend supporters throughout the Gulf Region.[109] This is another example of the pragmatic bend in HAMAS. The PLO openly supported the Iraqi regime. HAMAS, realizing that there was little to be gained, avoided public pronouncements. The PLO's missteps may have created an interest within HAMAS to seize leadership of the Palestinians from the PLO.

Diametrically opposed to negotiations, HAMAS would be faced with the challenge of not only Israeli oppression but also the fact that for the first time the PLO would enter into viable negotiations with Israel in the talks leading up to the Oslo Accords. This further enforced HAMAS' identity as one of a resistance movement. Looking through the lens of this time period it is understandable why Israel and the West could not foresee ever having to work with the Movement. The defeat of Iraq, and the fall of the Soviet Union allowed the United States and the Western world to focus on establishing peace rather than fighting a proxy war in the Palestinian territories.[110] HAMAS countered the peace process by pointing to the perception that the Palestinians seemed to give up much more than they gained from negotiations. They continued to portray themselves as the true resistance movement by provoking Israel and stepping up attacks on soldiers and civilians. Their aim was to disrupt peace talks and make the PLO / PA appear ineffectual.[111] Eventually Israel responded by deporting several hundred HAMAS leaders and supporters to Marj al-Zohour in South Lebanon.[112] This provided a golden opportunity, thrusting the Resistance into the international spotlight and giving them access to the global media. Well educated and articulate, the

---

[108] Ahmad, 40-41.

[109] Ibid, 44.

[110] Kepel, 323

[111] Ibid, 326.

[112] Ahmad, 76.

leadership engaged with media and the international community during their exile, spreading a more palatable version of their message to a global audience.[113] Desperate to regain relevance, Arafat began talks with Israel that would eventually lead to the Oslo Declaration.[114] This period seems to be the time when HAMAS realized that advantage could be gained by working through an established system of local elections and participation in international conferences.

The Oslo Declaration created a relatively autonomous Palestine effectively ending the First *Intifada.* This created several problems for HAMAS.[115] They had to choose between continuing to fight Israel in the name of their ultimate objective or working within the settlement in order to provide relatively peace and calm that many of their supporters yearned for.[116] With the transformation of the PLO from terrorist group to legitimate governing authority in the form of the Palestinian National Authority (PA), HAMAS moved to the forefront of the violent opposition to Israel.[117] HAMAS reacted by launching suicide attacks against Israel and by participating the Popular Arab and Islamic Conference in Khartoum, Sudan.[118] Organizations opposed to Oslo rallied to express their displeasure with the Accords, the PA, and Israel at this conference. The PA now had the responsibility to establish law in order in the territories. This also included the violent suppression and jailing of resistance movements such as HAMAS. The PA police, recruited from amongst the people, proved to be much more effective than the Israelis at disrupting HAMAS networks.

The PLO's transition to the PA solidified HAMAS' perception that the PLO was lost as a potential ally in its resistance to Israel. For the first time in its existence, HAMAS was losing support from two of its key constituencies, the religious middle class and the disaffected youth.[119] This caused the

---

[113] Ahmad, 82 and Kepel, 327.

[114] Kepel, 327.

[115] Alexander, 2.

[116] Kepel, 328.

[117] Ayoob, 120.

[118] Barsky, 5.

[119] Kepel, 330

leaders of HAMAS to reach out to the PA, only to be rebuffed.[120] This attempt to settle with the PA marked a definitive shift in the normative structure of HAMAS. Despite the fact that the PLO had violated a behavioral norm of the Resistance Movement, HAMAS still showed a willingness to reach out to them in order to become a part of the PA. Previously the organization had stated that its goals could only achieve its goals through Jihad. It also stated that anyone who had left this struggle was guilty of treason and an abomination to Islam.[121] The choice to reach out to the PLO marked not only a shift in choice of acceptable means but also a potential change in the normative structure of HAMAS. This may also indicate a change in interests. Priorities seemed to shift from the violent destruction of Israel to the leadership of the Palestinian people. The willingness to work with the PLO, despite their engagement with Israel, seems to indicate a moderation in their normative structure. The emphasis was on pragmatism and power rather than Islamic revolution and the establishment of a Palestinian state under Sharia.

The assassination of Prime Minister Rabin, targeted killing of HAMAS bomb maker Yahya Ayyache, and the cycle of suicide attacks followed by Israeli reaction, only served to weaken the Resistance Movement and plunge the Palestinian people into deeper despair.[122] HAMAS was weakened, the PA impotent, and the hardliners in Israel were gaining strength. However, events seemed to conspire to bring HAMAS back to the fore. Ariel Sharon, in a maneuver to leverage himself into the seat of prime minister, visited the *Al Aqsa* Mosque in Jerusalem.[123] This perceived insult combined with frustration with the fruitless peace process pushed the Palestinian people once more into the streets. The Second *Intifada*, or as it is more commonly called, the *al Aqsa Intifada* was born.[124]

---

[120] Ibid.

[121] Farmer, 97.

[122] Kepel, 332.

[123] Ibid.

[124] Considerable controversy surrounds the beginnings of the *al Aqsa Intifada* and what or who caused a protest to transition to full blown civil unrest.

During the First *Intifada*, civilians were often the target or victims of the violence between Israel and various groups in the Palestinian territories. During the *al Aqsa Intifada*, groups, particularly HAMAS, began to focus their attacks on civilian targets inside Israel. HAMAS formed its military wing, the *Iz Al-Din Al-Qassam* Brigades.[125] This organization attacked both civilian and military targets. HAMAS had taken a page from the Hezbollah, and they had the backing from their *Salafist* religious scholars.[126] The Israeli response to these attacks was brutal but effective, the introduction of precision munitions allowed them to decimate the critical leadership infrastructure of not only HAMAS but also the PA. HAMAS operations shifted from assassination and kidnapping of primarily military targets, to indiscriminate suicide attacks with the sole focus of killing Israelis. The *al Aqsa Intifada* seems to mark a shift back to the normative structure established in the *Covenant*.

Al Qaeda's attacks on the United States on September 11, 2001 had multiple effects on the Palestinian territories in general and HAMAS in particular. It allowed the Israelis to more openly attack resistance groups, as Ariel Sharon was able to effectively link Palestinian nationalism with the US war on terror.[127] The United States' perceived an increased connection between themselves and Israel. They both shared a status as victims of attacks from Islamic terrorist groups who were engaged in an existential struggle.[128] Also, as a result of the attacks, laws were enacted that allowed US law enforcement to more aggressively take action against funding associated with terrorism. The US shut down the Holy Land Foundation and CAIR (the Council on American-Islamic Relations), two groups closely linked to HAMAS. This eliminated a source of funding and public relations for HAMAS and only deepened US suspicions of their intentions. Another effect of September 11 on the Resistance Movement is that its

---

[125] Ayoob, 126. Named for Sheikh Izz Al-Din Al-Qassam, one of the first leaders of the Palestinian resistance against the British occupation. See: Palestinian Academic Society for the Study of International Affairs, "Palestine Facts: Personalities: Alphabetical Listing," Palestinian Academic Society for the Study of International Affairs, http://www.passia.org/palestine_facts/personalities/alpha_q.htm (accessed August 3, 2008).

[126] Kepel, 333.

[127] Kepel, 334 and Chehab, 182.

[128] Arguably the perception of an existential threat was short lived the American public, however, for the most part, Israel's continue to view their struggle as a matter of life or death.

regional supporters became much more hesitant to support a group identified by the United States as a terrorist organization.[129] The September 11 attacks and the subsequent US war on terror shifted HAMAS' operational environment. Suicide attacks would no longer be perceived as a sign of how desperate the situation in Palestine had become. Instead these attacks would be perceived as a philosophical link to AQ. Four years later, HAMAS would be perceived as so weak and peripheral that Mahmoud Abbas would allow them to participate in elections for the Palestinian Legislature.

Four major events seem to have shaped the normative structure of HAMAS since the publication of the *Covenant*. Three of them occurred within the framework of the Palestinian-Israeli issue. They are the First *Intifada*, the signing of the Oslo Accords, and the *Al Aqsa Intifada*. The external event that dramatically shaped the Resistance's normative structure was the September 11, 2001 attacks by Al *Aqaeda* against the United States. The First Intifada served to reinforce the normative structures established in the foundation of HAMAS and codified in the publication of the *Covenant*. The religious orientation served to distinguish the organization from FATAH. Resistance against Israel and the provision of desperately needed social services were seen not only a religious obligation but also as a means to garner the support of the Palestinian people.[130]

The Oslo accords established the PA and thus FATAH as a legitimate political leadership in Palestine. This caused HAMAS to reorient not so much on resistance against Israel but more so on disruption of any negotiations. Oslo reinforced the religious identity of HAMAS and thrust it into the primary leadership role in resisting Israeli occupation. It may have also had the affect of establishing political leadership as a potential means to accomplish the organizations ends. The mass deportation of HAMAS associated leadership and intelligentsia demonstrated to HAMAS that politics and activism could win support and sympathy for their cause.

---

[129] Hassan A. Barari, "The Al-Aqsa Intifada as Seen in Egypt," in *Between Terrorism and Civil War: The Al-Aqsa Intifada*, ed. Clive Jones and Ami Pedahzur (London: Routledge, 2005), 98.

[130] Farmer, 97.

The *Al Aqsa Intifada* temporarily sidelined any moderation in the normative structure of HAMAS and initially served to reinforce the Movement's original normative structure. However, under Oslo the PLO was effectively sidelined as a resistance. They assumed control of the PA who was obligated to work against HAMAS. Survival again became an issue for the Resistance Movement. This combined with the establishment of the US led Global War on Terror created the impetus for change. Israel was now able to focus on two immediate threats, Hezbollah and HAMAS while much of the global attention on the plight of the Palestinians was diverted elsewhere. Another effect of September 11th was that the Israelis felt less restraint in their efforts to violently confront HAMAS.[131] Political participation and negotiation became more attractive as the very existence of HAMAS was threatened. A changed environment as well as new opportunities created conditions that would push HAMAS towards a change in normative structure.

HAMAS Legislative Majority and Governance – A Changing Normative Structure and the Role of the International Community

President Mahmoud Abbas allowed HAMAS to participate in the Palestinian Legislative elections in an attempt to co-opt them through nominal representation. Participation would eventually force them to accept the Palestinian Authority's agenda.[132] The 2005-2006 election campaign marks the first occasion that HAMAS participated in a process enabled by the Oslo accords.[133] In conjunction with an agreement to participate in the elections, HAMAS established a *tahidiyya* (calm) in March 2005 with Israel, intentionally avoiding conflict during the campaign and electoral process.[134] The Resistance

---

[131] Barari, 99-100.

[132] Mohammed Yaghi, "Understanding the Hamas Agenda," in *Hamas Triumphant: Implications for Security, Politics, Economy, and Strategy*, Policy Focus no. 53. ed. Robert Satloff (Washington: The Washington Institute for Near East Policy, February 2006), 6.

[133] Zaki Chehab, *Inside Hamas: The Untold Story of the Militant Islamic Movement* (New York: Nation Books), 4 and Ayoob, 126. As previously stated, HAMAS had participated in previous elections but those were of a local nature.

[134] Christopher Hamilton, Jamie Chosak, and Joseph Solomon, "Maintaining the Tahdiyya: Hurdles for Hamas's Postelection Military Strategy," in *Hamas Triumphant: Implications for Security, Politics, Economy, and*

Movement saw the displeasure in the Palestinian people with FATAH, and they choose to use the ballet box as a means to seize control from FATAH.[135] The election results of January 2006 proved that Abbas' strategy was flawed. HAMAS' perceived weakness was illusory. The conventional wisdom believed that HAMAS would take seats from FATAH. Few commentators believed that the Resistance Movement would dominate the election.[136] This victory would precipitate a crisis unlike any seen in the Palestinian Territories since the First *Intifada*.

HAMAS achieved a parliamentary majority through their traditional base of support, the poverty-stricken youth, devout middle class, and the intelligentsia who provided the movement with much of its theoretical and philosophical underpinnings.[137] In power, the Palestinian people expected HAMAS to deliver on their political parties name, reform and change. Previously, HAMAS had been able to serve as an engine of reform by delivering services and acting as an alternative to FATAH.[138] The election marked a watershed event for HAMAS. It was the system shock that may have caused the organization to transition from the norms and identity of a resistance movement to one of a party in power. However actors and events served to reinforce HAMAS' previously held normative structure.

After an extended period of negotiation, HAMAS and President Abbas formed the National Unity Government. Immediately the US, EU, and Israel severed relations with the Palestinian authority. This decision doomed the government that was completely dependant on outside assistance to survive.[139] The

---

Strategy, Policy Focus no. 53. ed. Robert Satloff (Washington: The Washington Institute for Near East Policy, February 2006), 37.

[135] Ayoob, 126.

[136]. See Ben Fishman, "Hamas, Fatah, and Palestinian Politics After January 25" in *Hamas Triumphant: Implications for Security, Politics, Economy, and Strategy*, Policy Focus no. 53. ed. Robert Satloff (Washington: The Washington Institute for Near East Policy, February 2006), 6. HAMAS managed to take 74 of the 132 seats, FATAH took 45, and all others took thirteen combined. Even more stunning that the number of seats is the fact that HAMAS won more seats than any other party in eleven of sixteen districts, tied in two, and only failed to take a majority of seats in two. FATAH took all two seats in the Qalqiya District and the only seat in the Jericho District. HAMAS and FATAH tied in the Jenin and Bethlehem Districts.

[137] Kippel, *Jihad*, 325.

[138] Yaghi, 11.

[139] Chehab, 157.

US and the international community missed an opportunity by refusing to engage the Unity Government.[140] With more patience and a better understanding of HAMAS and the politics involved the West may have been better able to slowly push HAMAS towards moderation.[141] Instead, the international community in the form of the Quartet made demands that HAMAS would not be able to meet. Its demands included "… that all members of a future Palestinian government must be committed to nonviolence, recognition of Israel, and acceptance of previous agreements and obligations, including the Roadmap."[142] President Abbas illegally dissolved the National Unity Government and dismissed the legislature in order to get back into the good graces of the US and Europe.[143] Instead of exploiting the potential for modification or establishing HAMAS as an organization politically accountable to the Palestinian People, the actions of the Quartet and FATAH combined to reinforce the original normative structure of HAMAS. The decision to participate in the election and the subsequent victory seemed to indicate a moderation in HAMAS. The unrealistic demands of the Quartet reinforced the hard line narrative that negotiations were a waste of time and that organizational goals could only be accomplished through Jihad.[144] The actions of FATAH and the Quartet from 2006 to 2008 have been ineffective in dislodging HAMAS from power. The dissolution of the National Unity Government only serves to reinforce the Resistance Movement rather than undermine it.

Shortly after the elections, HAMAS, fearful of FATAH resistance to the new political reality moved to consolidate its power in Gaza. In the span of a month or two, they brutally removed any threat connected to FATAH. Executions, murder and assassinations of members of the FATAH were

---

[140] Cohen, Roger. "A Norwegian alternative to Bush's war on terrorism," The Daily Star (Lebanon), July 28, 2008, http://www.dailystar.com.lb/article.asp?edition_ID=10&article_ID=94563&categ_id=5 (accessed July 31, 2008).

[141] Chehab, 167.

[142] US Department of State, , *Quartet Statement on the Situation in the Middle East*, Sean McCormack - spokesman, January 30, 2006, http://www.state.gov/r/pa/prs/ps/2006/60068.htm (accessed October 11, 2008).

[143] Al-Haq, "Al-Haq Interventions to the President of the Palestinian National Authority and the Political Leadership of Hamas," Al-Haq, http://www.alhaq.org/etemplate.php?id=323 (accessed July 31, 2008). Only the legislature can dissolve the government or dismiss itself. See also Ayoob, 128-129.

[144] HAMAS, Article 13 and 14 and Ayoob, 127.

commonplace.[145] The *al-Qassam* brigades became the de facto law enforcement body in Gaza. Unemployment and infrastructure issues remain unaddressed. However, there was little noticeable political fall out for HAMAS. This is a result of the actions of the Quartet, Israel, and the PA provide it with an adequate explanation as to why the people of Gaza continue to suffer under their leadership. The strategy of isolation is having the opposite of its intended affect on HAMAS. Instead of weakening their support or causing them to change, HAMAS maintained its identity as a resistance movement and continued to garner support of the Palestinian people.[146]

HAMAS, FATAH, and AQ: The role of Contrast in the Normative Structure of HAMAS

It is useful to contrast HAMAS with both FATAH and *al Qaeda* (AQ) for several reasons.[147] FATAH, on one hand, serves as the primary competitor for Palestinian support as well as the secular alternative to a HAMAS that is clearly religiously oriented. Historically, FATAH has served as the "other" in the eyes of HAMAS; they are featured in the Covenant and the interaction between the organizations serves to define both. The comparison with AQ is also equally necessary. The United States' War on Terror has failed to distinguish between groups that use terror as a means regardless of motive. It may serve the agenda of some within the region and internationally to establish any sort of link between HAMAS and AQ, no matter how tenuous it may actually be. However, this examination will demonstrate that while AQ and HAMAS share some similar goals there are significant and perhaps unbridgeable differences between them. Despite the West's interest in al-Qaeda, FATAH continues to serve as HAMAS' primary other. The resulting conflict serves to define both organizations.

---

[145] Al-Haq, "Al-Haq", np.

[146] Ayoob, 128.

[147] The author acknowledges that FATAH, the PLO, and the PA are not interchangeable terms. However, FATAH dominated the PLO for over four decades and was in control of the organization, as it became the PA. When used in this monograph PLO refers to the organization prior to Oslo lead by Yasser Arafat. FATAH refers to the political party of Mahmoud Abbas, and the PA refers to the internationally recognized government of Palestine (which is run by FATAH). For a short history of the PLO, FATAH, and the PA see: As'ad Ghanem and Aziz Khayed, "In the Shadow of the al-Aqsa Intifada: The Palestinians and Political Reform," in *Between Terrorism and Civil War: The Al-Aqsa Intifada*, ed. Clive Jones and Ami Pedahzur (London: Routledge, 2005), 39-49.

HAMAS, ironically, was founded under some of the same nationalistic principles that the PLO originally stated in their 1968 National Charter.[148] They have worked with one another not only at the local level but also at the political / strategic level.[149] However, their relationship is one marked primarily by conflict rather than cooperation. FATAH is a secular organization, whereas HAMAS is strictly an Islamic movement. The former recognizes Israel's right to exist and actively seeks a negotiated settlement with Israel, often referred to as the two state solution.[150] HAMAS was founded with the goal to destroy Israel and replace it with an Islamic Palestine. Since it's founding, HAMAS has taken a violent approach to counter the Israeli occupation. Despite the common cause of the liberation of Palestine from Israeli control, there are three main reasons for conflict between FATAH and HAMAS. One source of tension is the role of religion and the state.[151] Although the PLO uses religious language, it is primarily, and practically a secular organization. HAMAS is outwardly religious, calling for the establishment of an Islamic state under *Sharia* law. The secular organization of the PLO naturally attracts the hostility of any organization that traces its roots to the Muslim Brotherhood, which was persecuted by the secular government of Egypt under Nasser and Sadat. Another source of hostility between the two organizations is geographic. The PLO and FATAH primarily draw their strength from the West Bank. HAMAS, on the other hand, traces its foundation and its principle source of strength to Gaza.[152] This plays on a tension that has existed between the divided Palestinian people since the state of Israel came into being. Both HAMAS and FATAH compete for a limited pool of both domestic and international support that is not easily distributed between them.[153] Nearly every major player in the Middle East has supported one side or the other. The final major reason for hostility is easily understood as a conflict

---

[148] Shaul Mishal & Avraham Sela, *The Palestinian Hamas: Vision, Violence, and Coexistence* (New York: Columbia University Press, 2000), 15.

[149] Levitt, 14-15.

[150] However, it should be noted that FATAH and the PLO's charter originally called for the destruction of Israel. Arafat renounced this position in 1988. See: Esposito, 101.

[151] Esposito, 96.

[152] Ayoob, 127.

[153] Levitt, *Hamas: Politics*, 116.

between parties that participate in any political process. This conflict will only serve to reinforce HAMAS' sense of self as one of a resistance movement. In the midst of a civil war it is unlikely that Palestinians will ever hold the government of HAMAS completely accountable for the miserable conditions in Gaza. This will reinforce the normative structure, interests, choice of means, and behaviors that are consistent with a resistance movement.

It is equally important, given the United States' "global war on terror", to contrast HAMAS with al-Qaeda (AQ).[154] While there is evidence that AQ has established a presence in Gaza there is little that points toward partnership between the two organizations.[155] The biggest difference between the two is their philosophical approach in creating an Islamic state. AQ has taken a top down approach, creating an Islamic state that facilitates the creation of the Islamic man. HAMAS, heavily influenced by its Muslim Brotherhood roots, takes the opposite approach. They believe that the first focus should be on developing pious Muslims and then the Muslim state can be realized.[156] The approach of HAMAS allows for much greater flexibility in adapting practice and policy to reality on the ground. This philosophy also allows for HAMAS to participate in elections, which are not valued for their democratic principles but instead as a means to realize the creation of a Muslim state. Both organizations support violent Jihad however, their take on the issue is distinguishable. AQ supports a global Jihad against the United States and Israel, targeting both military and civilian personnel across the globe.[157] Despite the use of similar tactics HAMAS, supports a jihad that is focused on achieving nationalistic goals and restricts its operations to Israel and Palestine[158] While HAMAS may make statements of support to other struggles, there is little support beyond words. The Resistance Movement has at times, been critical of AQ attacks.[159] AQ is

---

[154] Fradkin, 7-8.

[155] Hamilton, Chosak, and Solomon, 37 and Chehab, 189 and 192.

[156] Hassan Mneimneh, "The Islamization of Arab Culture." *Current Trends in Islamist Ideology* 6 (2008): 49 and Chehab, 190 and Levitt, 204.

[157] Ayoob, 21.

[158] Chehab, 196 and Ayoob, 19-21.

[159] Hamilton, Chosak, and Solomon, 39.

more concerned with the global Islamic issues of the body of Muslims (the Umma), while HAMAS concerns itself with the status of Palestine, the destruction of Israel, and the subsequent establishment of an Islamic state.[160]

HAMAS avoids working with AQ for practical/political reasons. The later has a tendency to subsume organizations. This would have two immediate effects on the objectives of HAMAS. The first is that their agenda would be diluted among the concerns of a global terrorist organization that is focused on confronting the United States. The other is that association with AQ severely restrains tactical options available, such as a ceasefire, available to achieve HAMAS' goals. Unlike AQ, HAMAS has chosen to participate in elections. This is because al-Qaeda does not philosophically except elections and HAMAS has a fixed geographic base from which to operate. AQ's Musab al-Zarqawi was highly critical of HAMAS' decision to participate in the Palestinian Legislative Elections.[161] While both organizations are religiously based, lay people lead them both. However, the AQ leadership in the form of Osama bin-Laden, unlike the HAMAS leadership, claims the privilege of issuing religious decrees in the form of *Fatwas*.[162]

While HAMAS and AQ share the goal of the liberation of Palestine, a *Salafist* orientation, and a willingness to use violence to achieve their goals; the two greatly differ in their norms, means, and behaviors. The former is willing to participate in elections, is nationalistic, and does not export its jihad outside the region.[163] The later has disdain for the electoral process as being un-Islamic, is Pan-Islamic, and works to spread jihad throughout the world. The differences between these organizations are unbridgeable except for short term and low-level operations. Al-Qaeda is more of a threat to then a friend of the interests and identity of HAMAS.

---

[160] Kepel, 26; Levitt, 220; and Chehab, 108.

[161] Chehab, 190.

[162] Fradkin, 15.

[163] Ayoob, 113.

Israel: The Out-Group's Role in Determining the Normative Structure of HAMAS

The fact that Israel serves as the object of HAMAS' resistance makes them a critical influence on the Movement's normative structure. The interaction between the two has been critical in the development of HAMAS' normative structure. The 2006 election may have presented Israel with an opportunity to modify this. Constructivist theory recognizes the critical role that outside actors can play in modifying normative structure.[164] Israel, however, along with the Quartet refused to recognize the HAMAS led National Unity Government and funding to the PA was cut off. This resulted in the near complete isolation of Palestine. This combined with the ongoing conflict between HAMAS and FATAH led to the dissolution of the government.[165] The isolation and embargo resulted in a divided Palestine that is no closer to a two-state solution.

Israel has several concerns with a government controlled by HAMAS. These concerns come from the fact that Israel still views HAMAS through the lens of a country committed to fighting a counterinsurgency. David Makovsky, senior fellow at the Washington Institute, identified five major issues Israel had with the inauguration of a HAMAS controlled government.[166] These concerns while understandable are not completely valid. Israel is concerned that the Resistance Movement will use their power to radicalize the Palestinian People. HAMAS was not elected based on their radical agenda, but because of their service orientation and the perception that they were above corruption, especially in comparison to FATAH. From its foundation HAMAS has established itself as an honest organization that holds itself above corruption.[167] Israel was also concerned that a successful HAMAS will empower and

---

[164] Berger, Thomas U. "Norms, Identity, and National Security in Germany and Japan," in *The Culture of National Security: Norms and Identity in World Politics*, ed. Peter J. Katzenstein (New York: Columbia University Press, 1996), 331.

[165] Pace, np and Associated Press, "Abbas Dissolves Palestinian National Security Council, Rallying International Support," *International Herald Tribune*, June 18, 2007, http://www.iht.com/articles/2007/06/18/business/mideast.php (accessed October 12, 2008).

[166] David Makovsky, "Israeli Policy and Politics in the Wake of Hamas's Victory," in Hamas Triumphant: Implications for Security, Politics, Economy, and Strategy, Policy Focus no. 53. ed. Robert Satloff (Washington: The Washington Institute for Near East Policy, February 2006), 15

[167] HAMAS, Article 36 and Levitt, 238.

inspire similar groups in Jordan and Egypt. HAMAS may inspire other groups in Egypt and Jordan. However, the social and political context that these groups exist in is vastly different that those facing HAMAS. While they may aspire to a electoral victory, there is little if any indication that this is possible in the near term. Another concern is that a successful HAMAS could work to radicalize the Muslim minority in Israel. As for this concern, researchers from Israel's Haifa University and the University of Texas argue that Israeli Muslims are more influenced by how they are treated by Israel than by religion or a sense of identity with the Palestinians.[168] Finally, Israel is also concerned that acceptance of HAMAS could erode international support for the current program of the two state solution. As for its effect on the two-state solution, this avenue of negotiation is virtually impossible without the people of Gaza, who are currently ruled by HAMAS. The economic embargo and physical isolation of Gaza has not brought FATAH any closer to reaching a final solution, nor has it brought HAMAS to its knees. Israel was concerned about their own ability to pressure a HAMAS led government economically could prove even more difficult than it was with FATAH. This pressure would undoubtedly lead to hardship for the Palestinian people. Israel concern for their ability to pressure HAMAS economically was well founded. Between 2006 and 2008, HAMAS has not been noticeably weakened by the economic embargo. In fact, HAMAS responded by bringing world attention to the plight of Gaza and has taken measures to counter the embargo such as the penetration of the barrier that separates Gaza from Egypt and increased use of tunnels in the Sinai Dessert.[169]

---

[168] Eran Zaidise, Daphna Canetti-Nisim, and Ami Pedahzur, "Politics of God or Politics of Man? The Role of Religion and Deprivation in Predicting Support for Political Violence in Israel," *Political Studies* 55, no. 3 (October 2007): 514, http://fw8pk7vf4q.scholar.serialssolutions.com/?sid=google&auinit=E&aulast=Zaidise&atitle=Politics+of+God+or+Politics+of+Man%3F+The+Role+of+Religion+and+Deprivation+in+Predicting+Support+for+Political+Violence+in+Israel&id=doi:10.1111/j.1467-9248.2007.00673.x (accessed October 12, 2008).

[169] Al Jazeera, "Angry Gazans Storm Rafah crossing" AlJazeera.net, http://english.aljazeera.net/news/middleeast/2008/01/20085251349446642.html (accessed October 13, 2008).

So far, Israel has aggressively used its economic power to leverage desired behavior from HAMAS. The Rafah terminal has been closed by agreement between Egypt and Israel.[170] This effectively gives Israel control over all goods flowing into Gaza since the only alternative is to move goods through Israeli ports. Israel has refused to allow anything but a trickle of goods to move into the territory controlled by HAMAS. In addition to this, Israel also collects duties and customs on imports and by agreement established in the Paris Protocol provides these funds to the PA.[171] Equitable portions of these have not been made available to HAMAS, despite the fact that they are the de facto government of Gaza. Israeli actions, reinforce an identity in the Palestinian people as victims of the Israeli occupation / embargo. That in term results in both an external pressure – the perception that HAMAS has no alternate except violence or capitulation – and internal / domestic pressure – the need to strike back at the occupier to maintain the normative structure codified in the Covenant.[172]

The relationship between HAMAS and Israel has an obvious impact on the normative structure of HAMAS. Israel's refusal to work with a PA that includes HAMAS, their economic isolation of Gaza, and their third party negotiations may tend to reinforce the identity of Resistance Movement rather than that of a governing party. While it may be the goal of the Israelis to undermine HAMAS these actions seem to strengthen them. The ability to blame Israel and FATAH for the economic plight and isolation of Palestine shields the Resistance Movement from accountability. HAMAS is now able to point to external influences as the source of misery in Gaza. Another possible unintended side effect is that these actions may be increased Iranian influence on HAMAS. As sources of revenues for HAMAS dry up, the importance of Iranian support grows. Realizing this, Iran may leverage funds to increase their influence.

---

[170] British Broadcast Corporation News, "Israel to Open Gaza-Egypt Border," British Broadcast Corporation, http://news.bbc.co.uk/2/hi/middle_east/4377776.stm (accessed October 8, 2008).

[171] Satloff, 7

[172] Ayoob, 130.

The US: Shaping Identity Through Action

The US relationship with HAMAS is neither complicated nor nuanced. The US State Department designated HAMAS as a terrorist organization in 1997.[173] Since then there has been a tendency with US leaders to lump HAMAS in with Hezbollah, treating them as interchangeable entities.[174] US concern over HAMAS' participation in the 2006 legislative election was so great that FATAH received $42 million to prevent a HAMAS victory.[175] The US reaction to HAMAS electoral success was immediate and hostile. Both the Secretary of State and the President indicated that working with a PA that included HAMAS was not an option. Written shortly after HAMAS's electoral victory the 2006 National Security Strategy states:

> The international community has also made clear that a two-state solution to the conflict requires all participants in the democratic process to renounce violence and terror, accept Israel's right to exist, and disarm as outlined in the Roadmap. These requirements are clear, firm, and of long standing. The opportunity for peace and statehood – a consistent goal of this Administration – is open if Hamas will abandon its terrorist roots and change its relationship with Israel.[176]

This unambiguous statement makes sense if one views HAMAS' interests as mere policy instruments instead of critical components of its normative structure. While constructivist theory recognizes that change is possible, it subscribes to the notion that change is incremental and consistent with the normative structure of the organization. US actions seem to reinforce HAMAS' normative structure rather than modify it.

After the formation of the National Unity Government, the US immediately withheld $250 million in aid from Palestine.[177] Once President Abbas dissolved this government, the funds were

---

[173] U.S. Department of State, "Foreign", np.

[174] Chehab, 218.

[175] Reuters, "U.S. begins $42 million program to bolster Hamas opponents," Haaretz.com, October 14, 2006, http://www.haaretz.com/hasen/spages/774570.html (accessed August 6, 2008). This has damaged both the image of the US, as the sponsor of democracy in the Middle East, and FATAH as an independent political party.

[176] Bush, 2006, 5.

[177] Chehab, 158.

reinstated.[178] The US has actively supported the development of capabilities of the PA, during ongoing hostilities between FATAH and HAMAS. Again, these actions reinforce the perception amongst HAMAS members and supporters that the US does not consistently apply policy to actors in Palestine. Despite the fact that there was on-going violent struggle between HAMAS and FATAH, the Quartet provided financial assistance to the FATAH controlled PA.[179] These actions may reinforce the notions within HAMAS that negotiations are a waste of time, outside assistance works against the interests of Palestine, and that the only way to achieve their ends is through *jihad*.

The US policy towards HAMAS may have served to more deeply imbed the organization's identity as a resistance movement. According to Mohammed Ayoob, author of *The Many Faces of Political Islam*, the pressure from the US and international community has "… hardened HAMAS's position while simultaneously discrediting its internal political leadership (which decided to join the PA government) in the eyes of its military wing."[180] In Ayoob's view, the actions of the United States are not having their intended effect. Instead of moderating HAMAS, US actions have served to reinforce the normative structure of resistance. In the past HAMAS perceived US actions as being overly supportive of Israel. Once elected, the US seemed to do everything in its power to undermine HAMAS. The strategy of the US-led Quartet isolates HAMAS, reinforces a normative structure that is consistent with a resistance movement, and pushes them towards Iran.[181]

---

[178] NPR, "Abbas to Bush: Time to Restart Mideast Peace Talks," NPR.org, June 18, 2007, http://www.npr.org/templates/story/story.php?storyId=11151699 (accessed October 13, 2008).

[179] Ibid.

[180] Ayoob, 128.

[181] Chehab, 220 and Patrick Clawson, "Pressing the Palestinian Authority Financially: Not as Easy as it Looks," in *Hamas Triumphant: Implications for Security, Politics, Economy, and Strategy*, ed. Robert Satloff, Policy Focus no. 53. Washington: The Washington Institute for Near East Policy, February 2006.

Iran – HAMAS: Reinforcing the Normative Structure of Resistance

Iran enthusiastically greeted the electoral victory of HAMAS as the "fourth in a series of Islamic

fundamentalist victories worldwide this year..."[182] The election and subsequent isolation of HAMAS may

only deepen Iran's influence on the organization. There is significant evidence to support the contention

that HAMAS receives support from Iran.[183] Documents seized in the United States and Israel indicate

that the Resistance Movement has received funds, training, and weapons since the 1990s. Links between

Iran and HAMAS are a source for concern for two primary reasons. Iran provides a link to Hezbollah.

So far, the relationship has been limited to training and technical assistance. HAMAS has trained in

camps run by Hezbollah in both Lebanon and Iran. They also received technical assistance in extending

the range of the *Qassam* rockets that were used to replace suicide bombings.[184] Iran may eventually be in

a position to demand a greater operational coordination between themselves, HAMAS, and Hezbollah.[185]

Second, Iran may be tempted to wage a proxy war against Israel in Gaza. It is commonly held belief

among regional experts that Hezbollah demonstrated that the IDF is not nearly as dominant in asymmetric

warfare as they are in the region's previous conventional war.[186] Even if they gain a nuclear capability

slowly bleeding Israel may appear to be an attractive option to a nation whose leadership has called for

the destruction of Israel. It is in the interest of Iran to maintain HAMAS' identity as a resistance

movement, and it will continue to reinforce this by providing funds, training, and material.[187] While there

---

[182] Kayhan, "Palestine votes for the Intifada," Kayhan, January 28, 2006 and Soner Cagaptay, "Reponses to Hamas's Victory from Israel's Arab and Muslim Neighborhood" in *Hamas Triumphant: Implications for Security, Politics, Economy, and Strategy*, Policy Focus no. 53. ed. Robert Satloff (Washington: The Washington Institute for Near East Policy, February 2006), 29.

[183] Nathan W. Toronto, *Where have all the Bombers Gone?* International Institute for Counter-Terrorism. ND. http://ict.org.uil/apage/printv/23874.php (accessed April 24, 2008); Chehab, 142-143; Levitt, 172-178.

[184] Michael Eisenstadt, "Regional Security Implications of the Hamas Electoral Victory," in Hamas Triumphant: Implications for Security, Politics, Economy, and Strategy, Policy Focus no. 53. ed. Robert Satloff (Washington: The Washington Institute for Near East Policy, February 2006), 43.

[185] Ibid.

[186] See: Ilene R. Prusher, "Lessons from Israel's Lebanon war resonate globally," Christian Science Monitor, May 8, 2007, http://www.csmonitor.com/2007/0508/p04s01-wome.html (accessed October 13, 2008).

[187] Levitt, 172 and 174.

clearly is a relationship between Iran and HAMAS it is difficult to determine how much control the former has over the later. In the past HAMAS has been able to hold Iran at arms length, eagerly accepting funds while shying away from taking direction.[188] However, as the need for funds grows, the ability of Iran to influence strategic and tactical decision may increase.[189] As the isolation of HAMAS increases its reliance on Iran will also increase. This may allow Iran to have unprecedented influence on the normative structures and thus behaviors of HAMAS.

HAMAS, Egypt, & the Rest of the Middle East: The Potential for Moderation

Egypt and the Middle East in general greeted the electoral victory of HAMAS as a positive development. The Egyptian government indicated that a role in government would serve to moderate HAMAS's hard-line stance on Israel.[190] This position is puzzling, given that Egypt actively suppresses the Muslim Brotherhood and prevents the party from openly running for office. Even before HAMAS came to power in Gaza, Israel has accused Egypt of turning a blind eye to the flow of arms into Palestine. Tons of weapons and ammunition have crossed the border. However, Egypt has arguably been the voice of reason in the conflict between Israel and HAMAS. The collapse of any government in Gaza would have a destabilizing effect on Egypt. They act as the indirect negotiator between HAMAS and Israel in an effort to avoid a destabilized Gaza.[191] Egypt worked with Israel to reseal the breech in the border fence on Gaza's southern boundary in early 2008. There response, however, was slow in coming. This may be regarded as an attempt to address humanitarian concerns in Gaza while avoiding provocation towards Israel. Egypt does not want HAMAS, a self defined wing of the Muslim Brotherhood, to have

---

[188] Eisenstadt, 43.

[189] Levitt, 174.

[190] Aaron D. Pina, *Palestinian Elections*, (Washington, D.C.: Congressional Research Service, February 28, 2006): 2, http://www.usis.it/pdf/other/RL33269.pdf (accessed October 13, 2008).

[191] Agence France Presse & The Daily Star Staff, "Fatah, Hamas in War of Words as Officials Head to Egypt for Factional Talks," The Daily Star (Lebanon), July 30, 2008, http://www.dailystar.com.lb/article.asp?edition_ID=10&article_ID=94640&categ_id=2 (accessed July 31, 2008).

free access to the Sinai.[192] Egypt and Israel have agreed to keep the Rafah border closed, due to mutual concern over the potential for weapons to flow into Gaza.[193] The actions of Egypt seem to have served as moderating influence on the normative structure of HAMAS. This has been accomplished by Egypt acting as an intermediary between HAMAS and Israel, demonstrating to HAMAS the utility of negotiation. This may serve to further empower moderate influences with the Resistance Movement. Many countries in the Middle East greeted the victory of HAMAS as a vindication against the corruption and graft of FATAH.[194] Simultaneously, they, with the exception of Iran, have embraced the two-state solution, and would like to see HAMAS modify its position. This in turn would serve as a moderating influence to other movements. Much of the Middle East has been silent on the Quartet and Israel's embargo of Gaza. Any expression of outrage over the suffering in Gaza has been left mostly to private citizens.[195] Syria, along with Iran, is one of the few countries to openly and enthusiastically embraces the electoral victory of HAMAS. Unlike Iran, Syria has little or no ability to affect HAMAS.[196] They can provide moral support but little else. Despite the fact that the Resistance Movement operates some of its organizations in Damascus, any change in attitude on their part would have little effect on HAMAS.[197] The position of most of the Middle East serves to help modify the normative structure of HAMAS. Instead of reinforcing an identity of a resistance movement these countries seem to embrace a shift towards a legitimate governing party.

---

[192] Peter Armstrong, "Your Questions: Ask CBC," Canadian Broadcast Company – News, February 4, 2008.

[193] BBC News, "Israel to Open Gaza-Egypt Border," BBC, http://news.bbc.co.uk/2/hi/middle_east/4377776.stm (accessed October 8, 2008).

[194] Specifically, Jordan, Saudi Arabia, Iran, Egypt, Turkey, and Lebanon as reported in newspapers of these countries. See: Bezen Balamir Coskun, "Hamas Victory in the World Media," Peace and Conflict Monitor, http://www.monitor.upeace.org/archive.cfm?id_article=338 (accessed October 13, 2008) and Cagaptay, 27-30.

[195] Middle East Online, "Arab activists accuse Israel of Gaza 'genocide'," Middle East Online, September 7, 2008, http://www.middle-east-online.com/English/?id=27769 (accessed October 13, 2008) and British Broadcasting Corporation, "Tutu: Gaza Blockade Abomination," BBC News, May 29, 2008, http://news.bbc.co.uk/2/hi/middle_east/7425082.stm (accessed October 13, 2008).

[196] Eisenstadt, 42-43.

[197] Eisenstadt, 43.

The two countries that appear to play a major role in the normative structure of HAMAS are Egypt and Iran. It is in the interest of Egypt to contain and moderate HAMAS, based on its own struggles with the Muslim Brotherhood. This seems to have some effect on HAMAS. Through Egypt HAMAS has established a temporary peace treaty with Israel as well as begun to negotiate prisoner exchanges. Iran on the other hand seems to want to use HAMAS as a proxy in its conflict with the West and Israel. Historically HAMAS has resisted outside control, however as the situation in Gaza grows more desperate Iran's influence may grow.

Interests - From Revolution to Political Power

As HAMAS has transitioned from resistance movement, to political party, to ruling party some of its interests have changed while others have been modified. The primary interest of HAMAS is embedded in its identity. Their ultimate goal is the creation of an Islamic state ruled by *Sharia* in Palestine. HAMAS views Palestine as the entirety of the state of Israel.[198] This is the ultimate and defining goal of the organization. However, the constructivist approach argues that given proper conditions the normative structure can change.[199] As HAMAS transitions from resistance movement to governing body, many of its immediate objectives may change. HAMAS, the resistance group, was able to focus solely on the maintenance of the organization and the continued resistance of the state of Israel. Social services were additive to these interests, as they served to maintain the organization by garnering support and building a recruit pool. As a government, the expectations of the people will change and this domestic concern may change the nature of HAMAS. The provision of services shifts from something provided by HAMAS in lieu of the incompetent PA and becomes an expectation. In Gaza, HAMAS, not the PA, is now expected to provide all essential services. Economic viability in Gaza is now a critical concern to the party. Along these lines, HAMAS wants to open the Rafah Terminal Crossing (the only

---

[198] Ahmad, 76.

[199] Berger, 330-331. Berger argues that defeat in WWII was in itself insufficient cause for change in Japanese and German political-military culture, but that this defeat opened a window of opportunity for the inculcation of values that moved both of these societies from a militaristic culture to one of relative passivity.

border crossing between the Gaza strip and Egypt).[200] This, it is believed, will lead to increased economic viability and a return of ability to provide basic needs / services to the people. Other interests include physically connecting Gaza to the West Bank.[201] Although interest in this has diminished as conflict between the FATAH and HAMAS has increased, in the long term it is still a necessary part of governing the entirety of Palestine.[202] As a governing body in power, HAMAS now has the interest of maintaining itself in power. This decreases the likelihood that many of the measures often associated with *Sharia* in the West will be immediately implemented in Gaza. Also, this concern for power seems to have manifested itself in the establishment of a long-term cease-fire with Israel as a means to bring security to the people of Gaza. This agreement is referred to as a *Hudna* and is an implicit recognition of Israel. According to Jonathan D. Halevi, a senior researcher of the Middle East and radical Islam at the Jerusalem Center for Public Affairs, "a *hudna* implies recognition of the other party's actual existence, without acknowledging its legitimacy."[203] In the past, HAMAS has entered into *tahdiya* (calm) with Israel. According to HAMAS leader Khaled Mashaal a *tahdiya* is "a tactic in conflict management and a phase in the framework of the resistance." While a *hudna* is not recognition of Israel's right to exist, it is clearly indicative of a shift in the normative structure of HAMAS. The change in the normative structure and interests of HAMAS seems to indicate a potential change in means selection and as a result behavior.

---

[200] Agence France Presse & The Daily Star Staff, np.

[201] Robert Satloff, A Primer on Hamas: Origins, Tactics, Strategy, and Response," in *Hamas Triumphant: Implications for Security, Politics, Economy, and Strategy*, Policy Focus no. 53. ed. Robert Satloff (Washington: The Washington Institute for Near East Policy, February 2006), 6.

[202] William A. Orme Jr., "A Link That Drives Palestinians Apart," The World, New York Times, October 31, 1999, http://query.nytimes.com/gst/fullpage.html?res=9406E5DC163BF932A05753C1A96F958260&sec=&spon=&page wanted=all (accessed October 13, 2008).

[203] Jonathan D. Halevi, "The Hamas Interest in the Tahdiya (Temporary Truce) with Israel," Middle East Strategic Information – The Jerusalem Center for Public Affairs, June 24, 2008, http://www.mesi.org.uk/ViewBlog.aspx?ArticleId=24 (accessed October 13, 2008).

Means – Evidence of Moderation in the Normative Structure of HAMAS

HAMAS has used varied means to accomplish their ultimate goal of the establishment of an Islamic State in place of Israel. Since the 2006 election they chose to negotiate a truce with the State of Israel while continuing to fight an undeclared civil war against FATAH. While capable of providing substantial resistance to an Israeli incursion into Gaza, HAMAS has realized that they would be ill served by a fight with Israel. The truce between Israel and HAMAS is purely a utilitarian one on the part of both parties.[204] The failed Lebanon invasion left Israel unenthusiastic about a potential invasion of Gaza. HAMAS is unsure that it could survive an attempt at regime change by the Israelis. Both sides are eager to see the destruction of the other, however, in the immediate future accommodation is likely to replace confrontation. The truce is consistent with the Islamic identity of HAMAS and with Islamic law that allows for temporary truces when one is too weak to defeat an enemy.

It is likely that HAMAS will continue to use violence as a political tool; this is consistent with their identity, as established by the Covenant. What is unusual is that since the 2006 election much of the violence is focused against FATAH. The use of this once unacceptable means may be based on HAMAS' perception that FATAH robbed it of its rightful place as rulers of the whole of Palestine.

Given that HAMAS remains isolated and in power in Gaza, the armed groups associated with them will probably continue to provide their version of law and order. This may continue to reinforce the normative structures of a resistance movement. These groups tend to contain the more militant / extreme elements of HAMAS. Under the National Unity Government there were initial conversations about rolling these elements into the PA's police force. This may have served to moderate the armed groups and HAMAS as a whole. The dissolution of the National Unity Government eliminated this as a possibility.

---

[204] See Footnote 28

Behaviors – The Results of a Changing Normative Structure

The election of HAMAS may influence the organization to modify positions and tactics that were acceptable as a resistance organization but may not be realistic as a governing party. Despite the fact that the National Unity Government was short lived, it is critical to examine HAMAS' behavior as the de facto government of Gaza. The transition to an Islamic state and implementation of *Sharia* law appears to have been delayed by HAMAS. Instead, HAMAS seems to have established a civil government in Gaza that draws on Islam as a source of authority (*marja'iyyah*) rather than as a source of divine rule (*hakimiyyah*).[205] There is the pressure on HAMAS to remain relevant in terms of the resistance while there is now the added pressure to bring closure to the conflict with Israel. On the tactical level this internal conflict has been born out in the transition from suicide bombings to rocket attacks as terror techniques.[206] Starting in 2005, HAMAS turned away from the practice of suicide bombings and adopted in its place rocket attacks. Both practices are proven to be highly ineffective, in terms of killing and in terms of spreading mass terror. However, HAMAS does seem to feel pressure to remain relevant in the struggle against Israel.[207] The choice of rocket attacks is a strategic compromise that seems to indicate a shift in identity and a potential area to build momentum towards moderation.

HAMAS has attempted to strike a careful balance between governance and its resistance credo. The *Hudna* seems to have been adopted in order to buy time for the organization to improve and subsequently maintain its power base.[208] The struggle with FATAH can be viewed in a similar manner. It is difficult to pinpoint the precise moment or event that caused the conflict to become violent. Nonetheless, it has and HAMAS is ill positioned to unilaterally end the violence. While HAMAS has

---

[205] Altman, 32.

[206] Toronto, np.

[207] Ibid.

[208] The term *Hudna* is significant because the *Koran* records that Mohammed entered one with the Jews while he was alive. The arrangement was one of convenience for both parties. In the Koran the Jews broke then treaty and were subsequently wiped out by Mohammed's forces. See Footnote 28.

been effectively isolated from the world, FATAH enjoys the support of the international community.[209] FATAH feels little or no pressure to reach an accommodation with HAMAS. Again, these events work to build on the normative construct of HAMAS the resistance movement instead of HAMAS the governing party.

Recommendation

This recommendation will provide the following: an overview of the Quartet's current approach to dealing with HAMAS, an examination on why this policy is failing, and a recommendation on what the policy should be based on a constructivist approach to examining HAMAS. The Quartet and Israel have adopted a policy of isolation and embargo towards HAMAS and the Gaza strip.[210] This policy is designed to impress upon the people of Palestine, and particularly Gaza, that HAMAS cannot effectively rule and should be removed from office. The intent of this policy is summed up in the 2006 US National Security Strategy that requires all participants to renounce violence and terror, accept Israel's right to exist, and disarm.

This policy has failed to fulfill any of the above stated intent. Instead of undermining HAMAS and forcing it to change the policy of isolation seems to serve to strengthen the organization. The group enjoys levels of support similar to those seen during the 2006 legislative elections. Violence between supporters of FATAH and HAMAS continues and the suffering of the Palestinians deepens. The policy of embargo allows HAMAS to blame the misfortunes of the Palestinian people on the West and Israel. This has two effects. It reinforces the perception that Muslims are being deliberately targeted and persecuted. It also allows HAMAS to avoid accountability for the desperate situation in Gaza.

Even if the Quartet's policy worked as designed, the failure of HAMAS would not necessarily be a positive development. Groups who are waiting to seize power should HAMAS fall are not necessarily

---

[209] In June 2008 an international donor's conference pledged $242 million to support the development of police and judiciary capacities. See: Agence France Presse, "Fatah forces arrest 50 Hamas members in West Bank." The Daily Star (Lebanon), July 29, 2008, http://www.dailystar.com.lb/article.asp?edition_ID=10&article_ID=94608&categ_id=2 (accessed July 31, 2008)

more amenable to the West. Other *Salafist* groups such as *Hizb al-Tahrir* (The Islamic Liberation Party), whose views are even more extreme than those expressed in the Covenant, are gaining support in Palestine.[211] Continued anarchy only increases the attraction of extremist organizations and may embolden AQ, a group that is attracted to ungoverned / lawless space, to make a move to more fully establish themselves in the Palestinian territories. The failure of HAMAS could prove disastrous for the US and Israel as well as the people of Palestine.

A policy informed by constructivist theory would recognize that HAMAS couldn't simply recognize Israel's right to exist. The denial of this right has been fundamental to the Resistance Movement from its inception. While HAMAS may be capable of change, it can only be achieved incrementally as the identity of the group transitions from that of a resistance movement to that of a governing party. As Robert Satloff observed "The record shows that the few examples of cooptation of Islamic parties occurred only after decades of evolution in countries that enjoyed strong institutions, powerful security apparatuses, and a supreme guarantor of the sanctity of the political system...".[212] Until these institutions, apparatuses, and guarantors are built significant change may be impossible. Significant change however is possible if approached incrementally and accompanied by a significant state capacity building effort.

Instead of demanding immediate change of policy and beliefs, the Quartet and Israel may want to consider a policy that allows for incremental change. HAMAS has already exhibited behaviors demonstrating that they may be on a path that could lead to a changed identity. They have already agreed to a long-term cease-fire with the Israelis, attempted to form a unity government with FATAH, and have stopped the use of suicide attacks against Israel. Instead of focusing on recognition, the Quarter may be better served to accept a *Hudna* as a first step. There are three reasons why this may be the only solution

---

[211] Omran Reshiq, "Palestinian Hope Withers, Hizb al-Tahrir Flourishes," The Daily Star (Lebanon), July 21, 2008, http://www.dailystar.com.lb/article.asp?edition_ID=10&article_ID=94336&categ_id=5 (accessed July 31, 2008).

[212] Satloff, 8

in the near term. The ideology of HAMAS prevents it from negotiating away land that it considers sacred. Additionally, recognition of Israel's right to exist is also impossible for HAMAS based on its current norms. Finally, a *Hudna* is religiously acceptable to HAMAS and their supporters.

HAMAS and Gaza are facing a humanitarian and economic crisis. This crisis can be addressed by a series of actions. President Abbas should be encouraged two reform the National Unity Government. Israel should be encouraged to provide funds from tariffs and import fees in proportion to HAMAS. Finally, the Egyptians should be encouraged to keep the Rafah gate closed. This will give the Israeli some control of what is coming into Gaza. Until HAMAS is willing to reform and drop its call for the destruction of Israel, imports and exports must be tightly controlled. These actions may have a better chance of reaching the long-term goal of a two state solution. The *Hudna* builds momentum towards a moderation of HAMAS' call for the destruction of Israel. Participation in the National Unity Government could have several positive effects. It reopens Gaza to the benefits of international aid that could go a long way to alleviate the suffering of the people there. Participation in the governance of Palestine may also force HAMAS to govern more responsibly as isolation and embargo will no longer serve as a viable reason for lack of progress. Finally, it will shift the confrontation between FATAH and HAMAS back towards the political and away from the realm of physical violence. A moderate policy best serves the interests of all parties and is a more appropriate fit when HAMAS is viewed through a constructivist lens.

Conclusion

This mongraph used Constructivist theory to analysis HAMAS and to develop a recommendation for a more effective strategy for dealing with this organization. HAMAS is critical to the interest of the United States for several reasons. It is one of the few democratically elected governments in the Middle East. It also plays a critical role in the resolution of the Palestinian-Israeli issue. Finally, the United States dealings with HAMAS may set precedence for dealings with other democratically elected governments who are viewed as extreme by the West. The rise of religious influence in governance seems to be an enduring phenomenon in much of the Muslim world. The ability of the US to deal with this issue is a strategic imperative.

Constructivist theory focuses on the normative structure of an organization. A normative structure is the behavioral norms and identity of a state or organization. This theory is better suited than the realist or liberal approaches for an examination of HAMAS because it allows for an understanding normative structure, interests, means, and behaviors. This better informs decision makers and has greater predictive power than either realist or liberal theories can offer.

The constructivist approach has four primary limitations. The difficulty of clearly identifying norms, the ubiquitous nature of norms, and ability of norms to explain both continuity and change, and the issue of agency are among them. In order to identify norms an organization's history, writings, and interactions are examined. The ubiquity of norms is addressed by using Legro's test of codification, durability, and acceptance. The power of norms to explain both continuity and change is dealt with by examining the history of an organization as well as the effect of shocks on organizational behavior. The affect of agency is addressed in a similar manner; focusing on the patterns of behavior over the long term. The construct of normative structure consists of actor identity and behavioral norms. Identity is developed and moderated by the interaction of norms, domestic and international interactions, and the environment. Behavioral norms determine what is and is not acceptable. They bring a necessary level of predictability that is required for any interaction. The normative structure determines and is influence by interests, means, and behaviors.

An examination of the history of HAMAS, its founding documents, and its domestic and international interactions reveals critical issues that should be used in policy formulation. HAMAS is an organization that was dedicated to the formation of a Islamic Palestinian state that is governed by Sharia in the territory of Israel. The realities of political power and leadership may have caused HAMAS to redefine itself. This examination reveals several powerful norms that govern many of the organization's actions. HAMAS will not compromise on its ultimate goal of the establishment of Islamic state in the current territory of Israel. They are dedicated to serving the people of Palestine and will not tolerate corruption or graft. This is one of the primary reasons they were able to dominate the 2006 legislative elections. Also, HAMAS will accept outside assistance in any form, however they will not tolerate outside direction. This norm was established in its break with the Muslim Brotherhood and continues today with its resistance to direction from the supportive Iran or incorporation with al-Qaeda.

HAMAS' history shows that over time its interests have changed. Initially, HAMAS was able to limit its interests to resisting Israel and establishing the organization's role in Palestine. This, along with its association with the Muslim Brotherhood, provided the impetus for developing social service capabilities. Competition with FATAH pushed HAMAS into involvement in governance. Since it has gained legitimate governing authority, HAMAS now must come to terms with the reality of Israel and the challenges of governance. The changing interests of the organization coincide with changes in behavior. The organization that at one time insisted on the destruction of Israel and actively opposed any negotiation has stopped using suicide attacks and has agreed to a temporary cease-fire.

Thus far, the policy geared towards isolating and undermining the organization has failed to modify HAMAS' behavior. A policy informed by constructivist theory allows the West to take advantage of the propensity of HAMAS to adapt to whatever situation it finds itself. Instead of isolating HAMAS the Quartet should work towards including HAMAS in the process of governance and peace. This will allow for two possibilities. HAMAS could either fail on its own merits with the result of its removal from power via democratic means or it could succeed and slowly moderate its normative structure. Either outcome would create an environment where a two state solution is truly viable.

Timeline

1946 – Palestinian branch of the Muslim Brotherhood founded[213]

November 29, 1947 – United Nations Resolution 181 partitions Palestine into a Jewish state and an Arab state

1948 – Jordan occupies the West Bank and Egypt occupies Gaza Strip as a result of war with Israel[214]

1964 – PLO founded

June 1967 – Israel occupies the Palestinian territories

1978 – Yassin registers *Moujama* (the Palestinian Muslim Brotherhood) with Israel as a nonprofit organization[215]

1978 – Muslim Brotherhood established the Islamic University of Gaza[216]

1982 – PLO is expelled from Lebanon

December 8, 1987 – The first Intifada begins

1987 – HAMAS is founded by the Palestinian Muslim Brotherhood

March 1988 – Israelis destroy Islamic Jihad cells[217]

August 18, 1988 – The HAMAS Covenant is published

---

[213] Pace, NP.

[214] Nikki R. Keddie, *Women in the Middle East: Past and Present* (Princeton, NJ: Princeton University Press, 2007), 130.

[215] Ganor, NP.

[216] Gilles, *Jihad*, 152.

[217] Ibid, 154.

November 1988 – Palestinian National Congress (PLO) declares an independent Palestinian state & accepts the right of Israel

December 13, 1988 – Yasser Arafat delivers UN General Assembly speech calling for negotiation with Israel

May, 1989 – Yassin arrested by Israel[218]

April 1990 – PLO offers HAMAS seats on the Palestinian National Council[219]

1991 – First *Intifada* ends[220]

1991 – *Izz al-Din al-Qassam* Battalions established[221]

1992 – HAMAS established political and information sections in Amman, Jordan[222]

June 1992 – 418 HAMAS leaders and activists deported to Marj al-Zohour, Lebanon[223]

December 1992 – HAMAS kills five Israeli soldiers in one week in 3 separate attacks[224]

August 20, 1993 – Oslo Accords finalized

September 13, 1993 – Oslo Declaration signed in Washington, DC[225]

February 25, 1994 – Jewish settler kills 30 at Tomb of the Patriarchs in Hebron[226]

1994 – HAMAS adopts the tactic of suicide bombings[227]

---

[218] Yonah, 1.

[219] Kepel, 156

[220] Keddie, 131.

[221] Yonah, 1.

[222] Kristianasen, 21.

[223] Gilles, *Jihad*, 326.

[224] Kristianasen, 21.

[225] Gilles, *Jihad*, 327.

[226] Ibid, 329

July 1, 1994 – Yasir Arafat returns to Palestine through Gaza[228]

July 12, 1994 – PLO becomes the Palestinian National Authority[229]

November 19, 1994 – Palestinian Authority police kill sixteen HAMAS demonstrators[230]

November 4, 1995 – Right wing Israeli terrorist assassinates Prime Minister Yitzak Rabin

1996 – Elections for President of Palestinian National Authority and Legislative Council held, HAMAS boycotts[231]

October 1, 1997 – Yassin released by Israelis[232]

October 8, 1997 – HAMAS designated as a foreign terrorist organization by the US state department[233]

September 2000 – Ariel Sharon visits Muslim shrines, Second Intifada begins

February 2001 – Ariel Sharon becomes Prime Minister of Israel

December 2001 – US freezes funds of The Holy Land Foundation for Relief and Development due to suspected links to HAMAS[234]

March 2004 – Israel assassinates Yassin[235]

March 24, 2004 – Khalid Al-Mishal appointed leader of HAMAS[236]

---

[227] Pace, NP.

[228] David Samuels. "In a Ruined Country: How Yasir Arafat Destroyed Palestine." The Atlantic.com, September 2005. http://www.theatlantic.com/doc/print/200509/samuels (accessed July 10, 2008).

[229] Gilles, *Jihad*, 328

[230] Ibid, 329

[231] Pace, NP.

[232] Alexander, 4.

[233] U.S. Department of State, NP.

[234] Alexander, 9.

[235] Barsky, 4.

November 11, 2004 – Yasir Arafat dies

January 5, 2005 – Mahmoud Abbas (FATAH) elected President of the PA

January 15, 2005 – Abbas assumes office of the President

January 18, 2005 – HAMAS suicide bombing hiatus begins[237]

August 2005 – Israeli withdraws from Gaza Strip

January 25, 2006 – HAMAS wins a majority of seats in Palestinian Legislature elections

March 29, 2006 – HAMAS sworn in as government of Palestine[238]

April 7, 2006 – US and EU sever economic ties with Palestine[239]

May 2006 – US 2006 National Security Strategy specifically mentions HAMAS election

June 25, 2006 – HAMAS launches raid into Israel, killing two soldiers and capturing one[240]

June 28, 2006 – Israel invades Gaza

October 1, 2006 – HAMAS – FATAH conflict becomes violent[241]

November 26, 2006 – Israel announces cease-fire in Gaza[242]

February 2, 2007 – HAMAS overruns FATAH compounds in Gaza[243]

March 17, 2007 –National Unity Government takes office[244]

---

[236] Barsky. 2.

[237] Toronto, 1.

[238] Reuters, "Timeline – Key Events Since 2006 Hamas Election Victory." Thomson Reuters. http://www.reuters.com/article/topNews/idUSL1752364420070617 (accessed July 28, 2008).

[239] Ibid.

[240] Ibid.

[241] Ibid.

[242] Ibid.

[243] Ibid.

June 14, 2007 – HAMAS takes over Gaza.[245] President Abbas declares a state of emergency throughout Palestine.[246]

June 2007 – President Abbas dissolves National Unity Government[247]

June 16, 2007 – US lifts ban on aid to Palestine[248]

June 17, 2007 – FATAH-led emergency government assumes office[249]

September 19. 2007 – Israeli cabinet declares Gaza Strip an "enemy entity"[250]

January – February 2008 – Gaza – Egyptian boarder penetrated

February 4, 2008 – Dimona, Israel suicide bombing ends hiatus[251]

July 25, 2008 – Suicide bomb kills 5 HAMAS leaders, organization blames FATAH

July 2008 – HAMAS and FATAH conduct respective mass arrests in Gaza and West Bank

---

[244] Pace.

[245] Reuters.

[246] Al-Haq, "Al-Haq", np.

[247] Reuters.

[248] Ibid.

[249] Ibid.

[250] Al-Haq, "'Enemy Entity": A Deliberate Attempt by Israel to Obscure its Continued Occupation of the Gaza Strip," Al-Haq, http://www.alhaq.org/etemplate.php?id=334 (accessed July 31, 2008).

[251] Toronto, 1.

Bibliography

Abu-Amr, Zian. "Hamas: a Historical and Political Background," *Journal of Palestinian Studies*. XXII, no. 4 (Summer, 1993) pp. 5-19. http://www.jstor.org/view/0377919x/di009647/00p00027/0 (accessed February 27, 2008).

Agence France Presse & The Daily Star Staff, "Fatah, Hamas in War of Words as Officials Head to Egypt for Factional Talks," The Daily Star (Lebanon), July 30, 2008, http://www.dailystar.com.lb/article.asp?edition_ID=10&article_ID=94640&categ_id=2 (accessed July 31, 2008).

Ahmad, Hisham, A. *Hamas: From Religious Salvation to Political Transformation: The Rise of Hamas in Palestinian Society*. Jerusalem, Israel: PASSIA, 1994.

Alexander, Yonah. *Palestinian Religious Terrorism: Hamas and Islamic Jihad*. Ardsley, NY: Transnational Publishers 2002.

Al-Haq, "Al-Haq Interventions to the President of the Palestinian National Authority and the Political Leadership of Hamas," Al-Haq, http://www.alhaq.org/etemplate.php?id=323 (accessed July 31, 2008).

Al-Haq, "'Enemy Entity": A Deliberate Attempt by Israel to Obscure its Continued Occupation of the Gaza Strip," Al-Haq, http://www.alhaq.org/etemplate.php?id=334 (accessed July 31, 2008).

Arab World for Research & Development. "Results of an Opinion Poll: President Bush's Visit, President Carter's Visit, Hamas' Agenda, Evaluation of Government, and Popularity of Political Groups and Leaders." Arab World for Research & Development. http://www.awrad.org/etemplate.php?id=51&x=4 (accessed July 24, 2008).

Armstrong, Karen. *The Battle for God: A History of Fundamentalism*. New York: Ballantine Publishing, 2000.

Ayoob, Mohammed. *The Many Face of Political Islam: Religion and Politics in the Muslim World*. Ann Arbor, MI: University of Michigan Press, 2008.

Barari, Hassan A., "The Al-Aqsa Intifada as Seen in Egypt," in Jones and Pedahzur, 86-106.

Barnett, Michael, "Identity and Alliances in the Middle East." In Katzenstein, 400-450.

Barsky, Yehudit. *The New Leadership of Hamas: A Profile of Khalid al-Mishal*. New York: The American Jewish Committee, 2004.

Berger, Thomas U. "Norms, Identity, and National Security in Germany and Japan." in Katzenstein, 317-356.

Bjrkdahl, Annika. "Norms in International Relations: Some Conceptual and Methodological Reflections." *Cambridge Review of International Affairs*15, no. 1 (April 2002): 9-23.

Bush, George W. *The National Security Strategy of the United States of America*. Washington, DC. National Security Council, September 2002. http://www.whitehouse.gov/nsc/nss.html (accessed April 4, 2007).

Bush, George W. *The National Security Strategy of the United States of America*. Washington, DC. National Security Council, March 2006. http://www.whitehouse.gov/nsc/nss/2006/ (accessed April 4, 2007).

Cagaptay, Soner, "Reponses to Hamas's Victory from Israel's Arab and Muslim Neighborhood" in Satloff, 27-30.

Chehab, Zaki. *Inside Hamas: The Untold Story of the Militant Islamic Movement.* New York: Nation Books, 2007.

Clawson, Patrick. "Pressing the Palestinian Authority Financially: Not as Easy as it Looks," in Satloff, 56-60.

Coskun, Bezen B. "Hamas Victory in the World Media." Peace and Conflict Monitor, http://www.monitor.upeace.org/archive.cfm?id_article=338 (accessed October 13, 2008).

Eisenstadt, Michael. "Regional Security Implications of the Hamas Electoral Victory," in Satloff, 41-43.

Esposito, John, L. *Unholy War: Terror in the Name of Islam.* Oxford, England: Oxford University Press, 2002.

Brian Farmer R. *Understanding Radical Islam: Medieval Ideology in the Twenty-First Century.* New York: Peter Lang, 2006.

Farrell, Theo. "Constructivist Security Studies: Portrait of a Research Program," *International Studies Review* 4, no. 1 (Spring 2002). http://www.jstor.org/stable/3186274 (accessed July 21, 2008) 49-72.

Fishman, Ben, "Hamas, Fatah, and Palestinian Politics After January 25" in Satloff, 21-26.

Fradkin, Hillel. "The History and Unwritten Future of Salafism." *Current Trends in Islamist Ideology* 6 (2008): 5-19.

Fuller, Graham, E. *The Future of Political Islam.* New York: Palgrave Macmillan, 2003.

Ganor, Boaz. "Hamas – The Islamic Resistance Movement in the Territories." Jerusalem Center for Public Affairs. (February 2, 1992). http://www.jcpa.org/jl/saa27.htm (accessed May 7, 2008).

Gettleman, Marvin E., and Stuart Schaar, eds. *The Middle East and Islamic World Reader.* New York: Grove Press, 2003.

Gwertzman, Bernard. "Shikaki: Palestinians Support Hamas, But Most Favor Negotiated Peace with Israel" Council on Foreign Relations, (September 25, 2006): http://www.cfr.org/publication/11522/.

HAMAS. August 1998. The Covenant of the Islamic Resistance Movement. http://www.yale.edu/lawweb/avalon/mideast/hamas.htm (accessed February 5, 2008).

Hamilton, Christopher, Jamie Chosak, and Joseph Solomon, "Maintaining the Tahdiyya: Hurdles for Hamas's Post Election Military Strategy." In Satloff, 37-40.

Heffelfinger, Chris. "Hamas' victory and the future of democracy in the Middle East." The Arab Washingtonian. http://www.arabwashingtonian.org/english/article.php?issue=2&articleID=15 (accessed October 6, 2008).

Herzog, Michael. "Can Hamas Be Tamed?" *Foreign Affairs* 82, no. 2 (March/April 2006). http://www.foreignaffairs.org/20060301faessay85207/michael-herzog/can-hamas-be-tamed.html (accessed October 8, 2008).

Halevi, Jonathan D. "The Hamas Interest in the Tahdiya (Temporary Truce) with Israel." Middle East Strategic Information – The Jerusalem Center for Public Affairs, June 24, 2008. http://www.mesi.org.uk/ViewBlog.aspx?ArticleId=24 (accessed October 13, 2008).

Hopf, Ted. "The Promise of Constructivism in International Relations Theory". *International Security* 23, no. 1 (Summer 1998). http://www.jstor.org/stable/2539267 (accessed July 22, 2008).

Jepperson, Ronald, L., R Alexander Wendt, and Peter J. Katzenstein, in Katzenstein, 33-75.

Jones, Clive and Ami Pedahzur, eds. *Between Terrorism and Civil War: The Al-Aqsa Intifada*, London: Routledge, 2005.

Katzenstein, Peter J., ed. *The Culture of National Security: Norms and Identity in World Politics*. (New York: Columbia University Press, 1996).

Katzenstein, Peter, J., "Introduction: Alternative Perspectives on National Security," in *The Culture of National Security: Norms and Identity in World Politics*, ed. Peter J. Katzenstein (New York: Columbia University Press, 1996), 24.

Katzenstein, Peter, J., Robert O. Keohane, and Stephen D. Krasner, "International Organization and the Study of World Politics." *International Organization* 52, no. 4, International Organization at Fifty: Exploration and Contestation in the Study of World Politics (Autumn, 1998): 645-685 http://www.irchina.org/Katzenstein/KKK1998.pdf (accessed 15 October 2008).

Keddie, Nikki R. *Women in the Middle East: Past and Present*. Princeton, NJ: Princeton University Press, 2007.

Kepel, Giles, *Jihad: The Trail of Political Islam*, trans. Anthony F. Roberts. Cambridge, MA: The Belnap Press of Harvard University, 2002.

Kowert, Paul and Legro, Jeffrey, "Norms, Identity, and Their Limits: A Theoretical Reprise." In Katzenstein, 451-497.

Kristianasen, Wendy. "Challenge and Counterchallenge: Hamas's Response to Oslo". *Journal of Palestine Studies*. vol. 28, no. 3, (Spring, 1999) p. 19-36. http://www.jstor.org/stable/2538305 (accessed May 1, 2008).

Lebow, Richard, N. "Thucydides the Constructivist". *The American Political Science Review*, vol 95, No. 3 (September 2001) http://www.jstor.org/stable/3118232 (accessed July 21, 2008).

Levitt, Matthew, *HAMAS: Politics, Charity, and Terrorism in the Service of Jihad*. New Haven, CT: Yale University Press, 2006.

Lewis, Bernard. *The Crisis of Islam – Holy War and Unholy Terror*. New York: Random House Trade Paperbacks, 2004.

Lyberger, Loren, D. *Identity and Religion in Palestine*. Princeton, NJ: Princeton University Press, 2007.

Makovsky, David. "Israeli Policy and Politics in the Wake of Hamas's Victory," in Satloff, 15-20.

Mamdani, Mahmood, *Good Muslim, Bad Muslim*. New York: Pantheon Books, 2004.

Middle East Online. "Arab activists accuse Israel of Gaza 'genocide'." Middle East Online, September 7, 2008, http://www.middle-east-online.com/English/?id=27769 (accessed October 13, 2008).

Mneimneh, Hassan. "The Islamization of Arab Culture." *Current Trends in Islamist Ideology* 6 (2008): 48-65.

Moravcsik, Andrew. "Taking Preferences Seriously: A Liberal Theory of International Politics." International Organization 51, no. 4 (Autumn, 1997): pp. 513-553. http://www.jstor.org/stable/2703498 (accessed October 6, 2008).

Palestinian Center for Policy and Survey Research, "Press Release – Palestinian Public Opinion Poll no. 27." Palestinian Center for Policy and Survey Research http://www.pcpsr.org/survey/polls/2008/p27epressrelease.htm (accessed July 24, 2008).

Pace, Michele. "A 'Modern' Islamist Democracy? Perceptions of Democratization in Palestine: the Case of Hamas" Paper presented at the annual conference of the British Society for Middle Eastern Studies, Leeds, England, July 5, 2008.

Palestinian Academic Society for the Study of International Affairs, "Palestine Facts: Personalities: Alphabetical Listing," Palestinian Academic Society for the Study of International Affairs, http://www.passia.org/palestine_facts/personalities/alpha_q.htm (accessed August 3, 2008).

Pina, Aaron D., *Palestinian Elections* (Washington, D.C.: Congressional Research Service, February 28, 2006), http://www.usis.it/pdf/other/RL33269.pdf (accessed October 13, 2008).

Ross, Dennis. Forward to *Hamas: Politics, Charity, and Terrorism in the Service of Jihad*, by Matthew Levitt (New Haven, CT: Yale University Press, 2006)

Reuters, "Timeline – Key Events Since 2006 Hamas Election Victory." Thomson Reuters. http://www.reuters.com/article/topNews/idUSL1752364420070617 (accessed July 28, 2008).

Robinson, Glenn, E. "Hamas as a Social Movement," in Wiktorowicz 112-139.

Samuels, David. "In a Ruined Country: How Yasir Arafat Destroyed Palestine." *The Atlantic.com*, September 2005. http://www.theatlantic.com/doc/print/200509/samuels (accessed July 10, 2008).

Satloff, Robert. "A Primer on Hamas: Origins, Tactics, Strategy, and Response," in Satloff, 5-9.

Satloff, Robert, ed. *Hamas Triumphant: Implications for Security, Politics, Economy, and Strategy*, Policy Focus no. 53. Washington: The Washington Institute for Near East Policy, February 2006.

Shikaki, Khalil. "With Hamas in Power: Impact of Palestinian Domestic Developments on Options for the Peace Process." *Crown Center Working Papers* 1 (February 2007).

Spencer, Robert. "Mark Levine: Noam Chomsky as Rock Star." FrontPageMagazine.com. December 7, 2004, http://frontpagemag.com/Articles/Read.aspx?GUID=4F4BF775-1098-4A19-BBFC-C529E0AD76DA (accessed October 14, 2008).

Toronto, Nathan, W. "Where Have all the Bombers Gone?". *International Institute for Counter-Terrorism*. ND. http://www.ict.org.il/Articles/tabid/66/Articlsid/284/currentpage/1/Default.aspx (accessed April 24, 2008).

U.S. Department of State. *Foreign Terrorist Organizations (As of 12/30/2004)* http://www.state.gov/documents/organization/41055.pdf (accessed June1, 2008).

U.S. Department of State. *Quartet Statement on the Situation in the Middle East*. Sean McCormack - spokesman, January 30, 2006, http://www.state.gov/r/pa/prs/ps/2006/60068.htm (accessed October 11, 2008).

Usher, Graham. "Hamas Takes the High Road". *New Statesman*, vol. 133, no. 4696, (2004).

Walt, Stephen M. "International Relations: One World, Many Theories". *Foreign Policy*, no. 110. Special Edition: Frontiers of Knowledge (Spring, 1998): 29-32, 34-46, http://ic.ucsc.edu/~rlipsch/pol160A/Walt.1998.pdf (accessed October 4, 2008).

Wiktorowicz, Quintan., ed. *Islamic Activism: A Social Movement Theory Approach*. Bloomington, IN: University of Indiana Press, 2004.

Zaidise, Eran, Daphna Canetti-Nisim, and Ami Pedahzur. "Politics of God or Politics of Man? The Role of Religion and Deprivation in Predicting Support for Political Violence in Israel." Political Studies 55, no. 3 (October 2007): 499-521. http://fw8pk7vf4q.scholar.serialssolutions.com/?sid=google&auinit=E&aulast=Zaidise&atitle=Politics+of+God+or+Politics+of+Man%3F+The+Role+of+Religion+and+Deprivation+in+Predicting+Support+for+Political+Violence+in+Israel&id=doi:10.1111/j.1467-9248.2007.00673.x (accessed October 12, 2008).

www.ingramcontent.com/pod-product-compliance
Lightning Source LLC
Chambersburg PA
CBHW081417280526
45788CB00009B/3131